Rigorous Magic

Rigorous Magic

Communication Ideas and Their Application

Jim Taylor & Steve Hatch

John Wiley & Sons, Ltd

Other Wiley Editorial Offices

John Wiley & Sons Inc., 111 River Street, Hoboken, NJ 07030, USA

Jossey-Bass, 989 Market Street, San Francisco, CA 94103-1741, USA

Wiley-VCH Verlag GmbH, Boschstr. 12, D-69469 Weinheim, Germany

John Wiley & Sons Australia Ltd, 42 McDougall Street, Milton, Queensland 4064, Australia

John Wiley & Sons (Asia) Pte Ltd, 2 Clementi Loop #02-01, Jin Xing Distripark, Singapore
129809

John Wiley & Sons Canada Ltd, 6045 Freemont Blvd, Mississauga, ONT, L5R 4J3, Canada

Wiley also publishes its books in a variety of electronic formats. Some content that appears
in print may not be available in electronic books.

Anniversary Logo Design: Richard J. Pacifico

Library of Congress Cataloging-in-Publication Data

Taylor, Jim, 1964–
Rigorous magic: communication ideas and their application/Jim Taylor & Steve Hatch.
  p. cm.
  Includes bibliographical references and index.
  ISBN 978-0-470-02601-4 (cloth : alk. paper)
  1. Communication in marketing.   2. Brand name products.   3. Brand name
products – Marketing.   4. Advertising.   I. Hatch, Steve.   II. Title.
  HF5415.123.T388 2007
  658.8'101 – dc22

                                                                        2007004230

British Library Cataloguing in Publication Data

A catalogue record for this book is available from the British Library

ISBN 978-0-470-02601-4 (HB)

Typeset in 11/16pt Trump Medieval by SNP Best-set Typesetter Ltd., Hong Kong
Printed and bound in Great Britain by TJ International Ltd, Padstow, Cornwall, UK
This book is printed on acid-free paper responsibly manufactured from sustainable forestry
in which at least two trees are planted for each one used for paper production.

To Sophie
(SH)

To Tom, Joe & Amy
(JT)

Contents

Foreword

WHAT IS AN IDEA? WHAT KIND OF IDEA IS IT? HOW can the idea be used? Does it have range and longevity? Is it any good?

Rigorous Magic could easily have been titled 'Fragile: handle with extreme care'. In writing a book about communication ideas Steve Hatch and Jim Taylor have attempted to define the ephemeral and classify the abstract and in so doing provide a road map to all of us that consider ourselves part of the community that attempts to succeed in taking products and services to market.

Communication ideas in the broadest sense are the rocket fuel of brand marketing. In the absence of sustainable unique selling propositions ideas become the principal ownable asset in categories that are devoid of clear product differentiation in format or performance.

To quote John Ford CEO of The One Centre in Sydney 'We believe a Brand Idea connects your business opportunity with a cause. A Brand Idea engages people behind your cause. And a Brand Idea embodies a clear belief and behaviour structure guiding and inspiring all you do, ensuring business and brand work as one'.

As the challenge of marketing to ever more knowing consumers increasingly becomes that of establishing and maintaining positive brand perception this book is important as it focuses on an exceptionally valuable commodity and the application of that commodity to commercial success. Among its most valuable contributions is to focus on the idea itself rather than on ownership of the idea.

Too many factions from creative agencies to media agencies and brand consultancies not forgetting PR firms, direct marketing agencies and design consultants have expended too much of their energy into claiming the right of authorship of ideas. It is probable that their efforts would be better served in uniting around the task in order to deliver the ideas that elevate brand performance from the mundane to the exceptional. Jim and Steve also place great emphasis on the role of the client or brand owner and his role in the conception, development and exploitation of ideas and in so doing answer one important question and, covertly at least, ask another.

The question answered is 'who occupies the central role in integrated marketing?' *Rigorous Magic* makes it clear the obligation falls squarely on the client to act as the ultimate brand steward and it is their responsibility to identify and marshal resources which may not be neatly aligned in a single marketing services organisation. This presents a challenge for everyone in the value chain, not least the client himself as the art of 'getting the children to play nicely' is often far from simple. In the case of any exercise that requires the determination of right and wrong in an area that is inextricably bound with both subjectivity and creativity, those with 'creative XXXX' on their business card tend to push themselves forward and focus on the visual expression of the idea rather than the idea itself.

The question asked implicitly rather than explicitly is about the tenure of the brand stewards themselves. Given the extreme significance of ideas in driving commercial performance it seems surprising that businesses actively rotate key people away from designated brands at quite the speed they do. From the perspective of rapid learning and experience it is easily understood but there is always a suspicion that ideas and their expression are vulnerable when change is made as it is a place where apparent change can be executed quickly and thus a temptation is offered to someone who wants to make their mark. It is certainly easier to influence ideas than it is to re-tool the factory. At the very least the message to business is that the development and protection of communication ideas is a higher order function not to be tinkered with lightly.

Rigorous Magic is useful in its exploration of ideas in the broadest sense but really delivers against the development of communication ideas in particular which as Jim and Steve point out have the potential to energise brands and consumer constituencies and in so doing drive the value of the brand itself. Within the frame of communication ideas Jim and

Steve identify three key categories (and seven sub categories) which in itself helps the stakeholders to define what they are looking for and what their expectations might be in terms of scope and durability. Essentially these classify higher and lower order thinking. At lower levels we can only expect to impact execution whereas at the highest level – the brand idea – we can expect the whole behaviour of the brand to follow a new path. In the communications world this hierarchy or classification of ideas has in many respects followed the evolution of the marketing services gene pool.

In a period when advertising agencies led by advertising creatives dominated it was no surprise that advertising ideas dominated and also no surprise that many of these ideas were really tag lines dressed in the clothes of strategy. As media services developed as a competence at first within and now without the ad agency structure, ideas that involved contextual framework, symbiosis between message and environment and media platforms began to gain attention and traction. All these concepts are alive and operating in a media channel near you but today in an environment of fragmented and increasingly focused and expert services the hunt for the higher order brand idea represents the Holy Grail.

Brand ideas represent the zenith of opportunity as they create commercial value and they create an almost self sustaining ecosystem of ad ideas, executional ideas and activation opportunities and create territory for platforms that can be owned and leveraged over time. Jim and Steve successfully communicate this point with iconic examples like Dove that embodies a very high level brand idea that successfully touches the ground in every executional outlet from advertising to cause related marketing. Incidentally, Ogilvy, the creators of the Campaign for Real Beauty, would describe the notion as 'the big ideal' rather than 'the big idea'. A big ideal sits at the nexus of brand performance, consumer need and social imperative and that makes it very big indeed.

It's all well and good using examples that we all recognise but significant value emanates from the book as a result of the exploration of purely theoretical articulations of brand ideas that rate their potential and relevance and this among other aspects of the work really help to create an actionable codification of the category.

If there is just a single mantra to carry with you when you turn the final page it is that ideas may be born from inspiration but that all the most durable (de facto the best) are a synthesis of insight, creativity, brand understanding and judgement. This in turn requires a blend of skills of relative scarcity and a role for people who might not normally define themselves as an 'ideas person'. What is clear, however, is that all the players in the creation game have to commit themselves to immersion in the category, its trade environment, communication channels and in consumer behaviour if their contribution is to be of real value.

Finally a cautionary note. A volume as instructional as *Rigorous Magic* might inadvertently find itself in use as some kind of rule book and as a source of corporate and creative dogma. Nothing could be more dangerous than that, nor further from their intentions. The one certainty of today's consumer context is that constant change will require rapid refreshment of ideas and execution and there is a danger that brands and businesses can become enslaved by the very same big idea that was intended to be the path to liberation. Evolution in consumer behaviour does not stop and the advent of social networking and peer to peer transmission about brands and the world that surrounds them has created a fluidity that we have not seen before. It implies a relentlessness that needs to be matched by all of us who want and need to succeed.

Rob Norman
GroupM

Figure 0.1   Rob Norman

Preface

'R IGOUR' AND 'MAGIC' ARE CONCEPTS WHICH MAY not seem to go together. At least, not at first. After all, 'rigour' is for university professors applying the cold steel of logic to a doctoral thesis. It is for hard-eyed scientists analysing the latest set of research data. And magic? Well, that's just a bunch of silly tricks and cheap illusions, isn't it? Fit for nothing better than a pre-school kiddies' party.

The trouble is, nobody takes magic seriously these days and for that we blame Walt Disney. Wonderful though Disney movies are, they have done magic a grave disservice. In the cartoons we all grew up with, magic was always the lazy way out. A casual wave of the wand or a sprinkle of dust or a rub on the old lamp and . . . Shazam! . . . Salvation! . . . Redemption! . . . Your dreams come true! . . . Your wish is my command! But magic hasn't always been seen like that.

The first magicians were an ancient Persian priestly caste skilled in subjects such as mathematics and astrology and the interpretation of dreams. These 'magi', as they were known, first entered the Western consciousness as the three wise men of the Bible story. They were figures who commanded instant respect, even awe, wherever they appeared. They were men of learning, men of wisdom and, yes, almost certainly, men of rigour.

But hang on a moment. What, you may be asking, does all this have to do with communication ideas? Well, fifty years ago if anyone had told you that an underarm spray could be turned into an infallible aphrodisiac or that a smelly sneaker was a prestigious fashion accessory or that a cheap butter substitute could save your life or that gravy was a way of keeping families together, you would have laughed in their face. But today all these propositions have proved to be not just plausible, but profitable beyond the wildest dreams of previous generations.

Of course, the functional benefits of all products have improved greatly over the past fifty years, but that goes no way to explaining it. What really distinguishes the enormous power and profitability of a great brand from an also-ran is very simple: the magic of communication ideas. A wave of the magical communications wand over Axe made it the sexiest anti-perspirant on the block. It was a sprinkle of communications dust that turned Nike into a cultural phenomenon, that put Flora on the health agenda, that took Bisto into the heart of the British family.

But this was not shallow Disney magic. This was not about cheap trickery. Their successes were not about coining a clever phrase or striking it lucky or simply being at the right place at the right time. There was a rigour behind all these magical processes and it is this 'rigorous magic' that we intend to explore in this book.

Clearing the fog

Ideas are strange things. They can have incredible transformative power but our experience is there's a lack of understanding about what they are and how they work. Our motivation for writing this book came from a belief that communication ideas are the cornerstone of modern marketing but need to be far better understood.

When brands do have an honest to goodness fantastic idea, it's thrilling. But all too often ideas are loose and ill defined, often using alliteration or some other literary device to conceal the absence of meaning or real heart. More often still, a strategic idea is sold by presenting a great execution that's instantly gratifying but disguises the fact that the idea is a false dawn with a limited life expectancy or breadth of application.

A lot of great things have been written about ideas as concepts but there is less in the way of practical help in understanding what they are, how to have them and how to know if you've got a good one. What we wanted to do was to write a book that offered practical advice and techniques that really work, as well as inspirational examples of ideas in action.

People have been surprised that we were writing this book. We've had a lot of different responses from, 'But you work in a media agency!' to 'Haven't you got enough work to do?' to our personal favourite, 'I'll buy it!' In many ways, the fact that we work for a media agency and decided to write this book is the point. Why so? Because nowadays most ideas transcend executional disciplines. And for this simple reason, all agency types have an equal right to originate and lay claim to them. All agencies are in the ideas business nowadays. And within our own company, Mediaedge:cia, we take them very seriously and believe they are the fulcrum of planning and a core element in 'what we do'.

Communications nowadays is far more complex than ever before and picking a way through the limitless options has never been more difficult. We don't intend to go into depth about the social, media and technological causes of these new challenges, as so much has already been written, but it's clear that the value chain in marketing services has changed for good and having an understanding of ideas, their activation and their distribution is important no matter what kind of organisation you work for. By clearing away some of the fog that surrounds the topic of ideas, we hope to offer a point of view on how brands can win in the future.

Labour of love

Great ideas are hard work. Creating and thoroughly testing them requires not just imagination but tenacity, diplomacy and the smartness to know when you require a contribution from someone with a different skill set.

We have a lot of respect for the creative process. It's extremely tough to create ideas and it's hard to objectively assess the potential scope and power of the idea you have. This is one of the reasons for the mysticism. Ideas are hard to judge, particularly in the absence of execution. A couple of years ago we interviewed a range of industry figures from advertising agencies, media companies and brand consultancies about communication ideas and although they all had their own point of view on who is best placed to judge communication ideas, they all came up with the same answer to how you know if you've got a good idea. Kester Fielding, the Director of Global Media Procurement at Diageo put it most succinctly: 'Because it feels right.'

There's a reality in Kester's answer that's instantly appealing. To some extent we all know when an idea feels good. But what's the difference between bad and good? What's the difference between good and brilliant? And what are the different types of ideas that are out there?

In the footsteps of eccentrics

Bill Bryson's *A Short History of Nearly Everything* is one those books you can return to again and again. In its 515 pages, it covers, well, pretty much everything, from the primordial soup to the here and now. Reading it, we were struck by how much of our knowledge of the natural world today is the result of the efforts of a certain barking mad Victorian gentleman.

You're probably familiar with Charles Darwin and his most famous book *The Origin Of Species*. But another of his works is less well-known: *The Formation of Vegetable Mould,*

Through the Action of Worms with Observations of their Habits.

In this incredible book Darwin wrote:

130 pages on the habits of worms.

47 pages on the amount of fine earth bought up by worms to the surface.

54 pages on the part worms have played in the burial of ancient buildings.

29 pages on the action of worms in the denudation of land.

Another 46 pages on the action of worms in the denudation of land continued.

An 8 page conclusion with index.

This guy really knew his worms.

And he wasn't alone in his obsessional nature. There were plenty of men in the Victorian era (and a fair number of women too), who spent years of their lives, often in foreign parts, trying to understand the world around them for the 'greater good' of Queen, country and empire. The one thing they all had in common can be deduced from that special word in the title of Darwin's book on worms – 'observations'. By spending their time observing the world around them, they were able to identify the most minute differences between species and, in categorising these differences, they were able to understand how the world around them worked. They might have seemed crazy, but you have to admit there's something beautiful about their attention to detail and their unrelenting dedication.

Communication ideas are relatively new inventions but there are now enough of them around for us to observe, categorise and examine what is and isn't working in the marketplace. So, following in the footsteps of our Victorian ancestors and inspired by their diligence, we decided to dedicate our time to really exploring, deconstructing and categorising communication ideas.

At the heart of this lies an understanding of the different dimensions of ideas: the good vs. the bad and the strategic vs. the executional. Having read this far, you'd be forgiven for thinking that we're only interested in the more strategic type of ideas. Far from it, in fact we genuinely enjoy executional ideas. Execution is exciting, it's what consumers experience and see, it's what suppliers support and what sales peoples are inspired by. Execution is real. But like those obsessive Victorians, we've taken care to observe and understand that not only are there different types of strategic ideas but also a number of different executional ideas, some of which relate to each other, some of which exist on their own and all of which can benefit from being driven by a bigger strategic idea.

Who are we?

So, you might ask, why do we think that we've got the right to develop these theories and techniques? What places us in a position of credibility when it comes to assessing the world of ideas? Well, we've both spent a long time at the coal-face. In our careers we've worked in almost every category and have been fortunate enough to have worked with and partnered some of the most exciting clients and agencies around. We've had experience working with all of the different types of ideas we discuss in this book, sometimes as creators and sometimes as executors. We've experienced what does and doesn't work from both sides of the fence and from this we've been able to build a framework of understanding to categorise what's going on in the marketplace.

In all honesty, however, the real answer to this question is that we don't in fact have a particular right. Like you, we're fellow travellers who just happen to think that marketing is intrinsically interesting and that finding new ways to improve its effectiveness is a worthwhile way of spending time.

Acknowledgements

From the two of us:

It was Michael Jones, now CEO of Mediaedge:cia in South America, who put us up to it. Two years ago, there he was looking through a bible-like 160 page PowerPoint document we'd produced on ideas, when he remarked 'rather than producing such a long document, why don't you turn this into a book instead?' And so we decided to take him up on it, although with work pressures it took a while to get around to.

So thanks must go to Michael. But whilst he was the catalyst, there have been several other people at Mediaedge:cia who also helped us in different ways. Mel Varley and Tom George both gave us important support in freeing up our diaries for rare, brief moments. Nick Vale, who shared with us a lot of his views, particularly around the type of idea we call contextual frameworks. Charlie Wright and Joshua Rex, for their help editing. Nathalie Alfred for the last minute boost. And importantly, Rob Norman, now at GroupM in New York, who helped us on structure, was kind enough to write a beautiful Foreword for us, and in many quiet ways, was just incredibly supportive. Many thanks, all of you.

And in fact, we'd like to thank Mediaedge:cia as a whole, for the passion the company has towards ideas. It's great to work for a company that practices what it preaches and is so future-facing.

Over and above our work colleagues, we need to thank Wiley for their amazing patience with us . . . considering we kept them waiting for 18 months. Thanks Claire and Viv in particular. And then there's Charlie Hiscocks and Clare Abley at SABMiller. Charlie, many thanks for giving us the opportunity to play with the world's best train set, drink the world's best beer, and for basically being the world's best client. Clare, thanks for sharing your views on how to research ideas.

And at a more personal level . . .

From Steve:

To Sophie, Phoebe and Frederick. Sophie, in the time it took me to produce one book you gave us two beautiful children. Thank you my love.

Lastly to Jim. Mate here's to your energy, your intelligence and your refusal to put up with good when great is within reach. You're the perfect travelling companion and a great friend. Remember The Optimist and keep singing in The Ether.

From Jim:

Funnily enough, I'd like to also thank Steve for his friendship. Steve and I have endured the trials and tribulations of writing a book together, and come out smiling. No small feat in its own right. I'd also like to thank my darling wife Ali, for putting up with my tired grumpy self on weekends; and my three kids, Tom, Joe and Amy, who I hope one day will read this book and find it inspiring.

1

The heart of
the matter

It means I'm dreaming, like when I'm dreaming of horses. – Sarah, aged 4

It means you thought of something that looks in your head and you can try it and it might look good. – Noah, aged 6

It's something like a brainwave that you come up with, that's normally pretty good, but it can be pretty bad, that normally leads to a plan. – Oliver, aged 7

FROM THE EARLIEST AGE, WE ALL HAVE A NOTION OF what an idea is, whether we're able to express it clearly or not. We all see ideas as inherently powerful things that can galvanise and drive us towards action. But when we embarked on our quest to explore the nature of ideas, it seemed at first that we were paddling upstream. We spoke to lots of different agencies right across the board and, without a shadow of a doubt, they all pay homage to the importance of ideas as a driving force behind their work – be it a 30 second TVC, a promotion, a sponsorship property or an event. Yet there seemed to be a lot of confusion surrounding ideas. What exactly is an idea? Are there different types of idea? If so, what are they? And perhaps above all else – what the hell is a 'Big Idea'? It seems as if everyone has to have a 'Big Idea' these days – but how do you know if you've got one?

So on the one hand, there is unanimous acceptance of the importance of ideas, but on the other, there are different interpretations as to what actually constitutes an idea. But gradually, we began to see the wood for the trees. Slowly but surely, like sunbeams piercing the fog, we were able to place these interpretations and points of view into a hierarchy of sorts – a hierarchy that we believe for the first time introduces a level of simplicity into the seemingly complex and mysterious world of ideas, as well as answering many of those thorny questions.

Selling ideas

Ideas are at the very heart of marketing and communications. This may sound obvious, but there are many people in our industry who have only just woken up to the fact. And for some, it still doesn't seem quite right to be earning a living from something as ethereal, weightless and intangible as an idea. They'd much rather sell something that you can drop on your foot, like a reel of film or a poster or a point of sale display unit. Indeed, there was considerable consternation and debate when M.T. Rainey (of Rainey Kelly Campbell Roalfe) first championed the notion that agencies should be paid for ideas and intellectual property, rather than charging commission income. The debate still rumbles on to this day.

Although, when it comes to the communications industry, it has to be said that selling ideas is nothing new. The legendary JWT copywriter, James Webb Young, told this story in his book *A Technique for Producing Ideas*, published back in 1965. It's about a salesman friend who visits him in his office one day, in a state of high excitement. 'We are having a meeting today', says the salesman, 'of our entire western sales staff. Its purpose is to discuss how we can improve our selling. In our discussions we've tried analyzing the sales methods of other successful businessmen and among them we've been particularly impressed by the success of Mr Kobler in his selling of The American Weekly. After studying why he is so successful we have come to the conclusion that it all rests on just one thing – he doesn't sell space, he sells ideas! And we have decided that is just what we're going to do. From here on, we are not going to sell space. Starting tomorrow morning, every single one of us is going to sell ideas'.

And although that was only published in 1965, James Webb Young had actually been telling that story to students as long ago as 1939!

Skip forward to today and it seems that anyone and everyone is in the ideas game. Research companies, brand consultants, PR agencies, promotional agencies, communication specialists, direct marketing agencies, media agencies, brand owners and even media owners are competing at a commercial level and battling head-on in an effort to win over the consumer through ideas-driven communications. But what exactly do they – and we – mean by a 'communication idea'? It is time to start working towards a definition of this key term.

What are communication ideas and what do they do?

'Communication idea' is a term that most people are comfortable with and it's broad enough to act as an umbrella for the many different kinds of concepts that we'll encounter in this book – from the so-called 'Big Idea' to the short term executional 'whizz-bang'. But what exactly do we mean by the term? There are as many definitions of 'communication idea' as there are organisations competing in this space. And when we look at the definition of a communication idea, it's important to try to differentiate (a little) between what they are and what they do.

So what are they?

Marc Earls, formerly of St Luke's and Ogilvy, told us that 'A communication idea is a construct that lies behind not just the communications, the paid-for communications, but a construct that lies at the heart of the company's explanation of who it is and what it does – to itself, if to nobody else'.

From our own side, here is our definition: 'Communication ideas are constructs that a brand uses as a foundation or "stepping stone" to help express itself'. Or, to put it another way, they are the bridge between the somewhat ethereal notion of a brand essence and what consumers see and experience in real life.

And this distinction between communication idea and brand essence is an important one, because the two are quite different. An essence is the brand's still point in a turning world. Brand essences are as silent and unchanging as the ancient heads on Easter Island. Communications ideas, on the other hand, are alive and buzzing with energy; they are the USB ports that brands use to plug directly into the world around them in a meaningful and focused way.

And looking now at the flip side of the coin: what do they do?

Well, they do a number of highly valuable things.

Julian Saunders of The Joined Up Company feels they do two basic things: 'They help an organisation organise what it does and they help plant a thought in the consumer's mind that's bigger than a single execution'.

This is fine, but it's *the way* that ideas plant a thought in consumer's minds which is important.

Because they do so in a way that is highly engaging. This is derived from two things. The energy inherent in the idea. And the emotional quality of the idea. To quote Dan Wieden, of Wieden and Kennedy, 'The only ideas that people really care about are those that have some emotional quality to them . . . that mean something in here (points to heart). Capitalism is an idea, it's a big idea, but it's not until capitalism is interpreted as freedom and you create a sense of what it means beyond my brain, that I start to give a shit'. The combination of the inherent energy in an idea, and its emotional quality, are what magnifies and drives a brand's communications both in the short-term and long-term. It is what cuts through. This is the gold dust of our industry.

So communication ideas have organisational qualities. They also plant a thought in a consumer's mind that is bigger than a single execution – and they do this in an engaging way by having energy and applying emotion.

But there's also a third important aspect to what they do, that Julian didn't put his finger on. And it's this. They help produce better communication plans. They do this by ensuring simplicity . . . answering, potentially, multiple communication tasks with a single idea. They also do this by ensuring more 'brand-centric' planning. In other words, they safeguard us from running off and chasing the target audience – trying to hold a mirror up to the consumer in our creative execution, if you will. Rather, they ensure we marshal our communication around the brand and what we want it to stand for.

All of this means that communication ideas are essential in the modern world. Certainly, brand owners now recognise this. They demand many things of their agencies. Advice, support, direction, assistance, value for money and strategy are all high on their list of demands. But above all else, clients want communication ideas. They want them because they know that in the ocean of bland brand marketing, communication ideas are an island of hope and inspiration. They want them because, when it comes to investment return, communication ideas are, without doubt, the most powerful weapon in the arsenal.

So all brands are looking for communication ideas, and very few brands choose to go to market without an idea informing its execution in the marketplace. Nevertheless, not all ideas offer salvation. One of the key issues is that nowadays, brands need to engage with consumers through-the-line. While the points at which consumers have the opportunity to interact and experience a brand are ever increasing, most ideas out there are simply not 'through-the-line' ideas, despite pleas to the contrary. Rather, they are advertising ideas – ideas that only really work above-the-line. Another issue is that many are simply not that good. Or if they once were, the client or agency hasn't had the nerve (or time) to execute them properly, thereby diluting their inherent value. Finally, there is a problem in that a lot of brands try to use pay-off lines as a form of 'ideas glue'. Now, if your pay-off line is the main idea, that's fine. But nine times out of ten, it is not an idea. 'Just do it' is not an idea. It might be a shorthand or dramatisation of an idea. But it's not actually an idea.

So what the hell is a 'Big Idea'?

One other question which is frequently asked is 'what is a Big Idea?' Shelly Lazarus, Chairman and CEO of Ogilvy & Mather Worldwide, contrasts a 'Big Idea' to a 'great execution' like this:

'The difference between a great execution and a "Big Idea" is that "Big Ideas" are media neutral and they don't require a construct to exist'. So, for her, a 'Big Idea' differs from a great execution in that it has an existence independent of its expression; a 'Big Idea' precedes and informs its executions which may take very many different forms through-the-line. But this goes for strategic ideas in general, doesn't it?

We believe that a Big Idea is simply the central, dominant idea. In other words it's the idea that is the driver of things. It can be a strategic, media-neutral idea. But it can equally be an advertising idea.

To illustrate this, let's look at one often-quoted example of a 'Big Idea' – the one used by Walkers Crisps as the basis of its long-running campaign. It is based on the premise that these crisps (potato chips) are so delicious that even famously nice people can be tempted to steal them from children. It was first used in a TV campaign in the UK back in 1995, featuring the housewives' favourite football star Gary Lineker as the crisp thief and it proved so successful that it is still running today, with a slightly greyer Mr Lineker still in the lead role. And Walkers' parent, Pepsico, has exported the premise to many other crisp markets around the world. For example, in South Africa, the Lineker role is taken by Rugby World Cup-winning captain and national hero, Francois Pienaar. In Holland, the crisp thief is played by the clean-living, family-friendly singer Marco Borsato and in Spain, it's film star and heartthrob, Antonio Banderas. So Walkers have clearly come up with an idea that endures over the long term and travels, as well as one that succeeds in selling a heck of a lot of crisps. 'A Big Idea' is certainly one way of describing it! So here the advertising idea is the driver of the communication. It's the Big

Idea. Not what is behind it, which is an emotional platform in the shape of 'Irresistibility'.

So in our view, 'Big Idea' is a term that is descriptive of status, not nature. But because people generally want to know the nature of a 'Big idea', this term creates confusion not clarity.

Why communication ideas are more important than ever

There is a general acceptance that the world of communications is changing as never before. Just think about your own experience over the last three years. Have you got a Blackberry? Do you use a PVR? Have you got broadband at home? Is it wireless? Do you use an MP3? Do you write a blog? Has the interlude between the writing and printing of this book meant that these disruptions are already passé and you're onto the next thing?

Enough people have written about these changes so many times that for us to set off on an extended argument on this theme seems a bit redundant. If you didn't know that change is happening, you wouldn't be reading this book. But just in case you're still unconvinced, let's select just one fact from the zillion that prove the point.

In 1998 in the UK, the number of television programmes with over 15,000,000 viewers was 227 (which represents a lot of Brits – not far short of a third of the entire nation, in fact).

And do you know what the corresponding 2005 figure was? Zero. It's easy to get bored by all the hyperbole around media fragmentation and the growth of technology, but something is happening here. It really is. And the trend is global.

We are now moving into a stage in marketing when consumers are going to be the key stakeholders in brand stewardship and they will want to pick up and play with executional communication components. They will want to participate, and disaggregate communication for their own ends. This is happening in many markets already and the trend will doubtless accelerate. And because the number of ways we can communicate is now almost overwhelming, it is more important than ever before to use ideas as a way of focusing communications and acting as a prism through which to assess channels, disciplines and executions.

All in all, the central, strategic communication idea, as the pinnacle of an ideas hierarchy, will carry an increasingly heavy burden going forward. It will have to be as hard as nails. It will need a quality of indivisibility about it, like a prime number. But, critically, in order to inspire communications, it will also need to be self-sustaining and inherently flexible.

As strategic communication ideas grow in importance, they will also be put under more and more stress. And there will be a temptation to sacrifice the energy in an idea for simplicity, so that it is clear and useable across geographies, and tough enough to withstand participation from the consumer. But in so doing, there is a danger that we may dumb down the ideas and dampen their energy, which is one of their critical attributes.

The fear of exposure

There are certainly many obstacles to overcome in the creation of an ideas-driven communications plan. These can basically be categorised as cultural, organisational and habitual. The modus operandi that is typically employed for communications development has been built up over more than a century of marketing experience. It is a part of our intellectual DNA. While many of the lessons learnt from all this experience still have resonance today, the marketing environment in which we compete has changed dramatically. Culturally, there is a misalignment between the models we use to develop communications and the marketing environment or landscape within which communication ideas thrive or perish.

As an industry we are inherently resistant to change, even after the change has happened. A mutual suspicion typifies the most common relationships between different agencies and sometimes between clients and their agencies, and it's easy to understand why.

In humanistic psychotherapy a lot of emphasis is given to the notion of boundaries. For an individual the absence of boundaries is very disconcerting. People talk of feeling exposed and vulnerable. This can result in extreme behaviour: anger, paranoia, depression, listlessness and violence may result as part of an effort to re-establish equilibrium. And when you think about what's happened to communications over the last ten years it is clearly evident that all of the boundaries have been removed. Like a client desperately trying to regain control, companies are fighting to achieve a solid sense of self. This wouldn't be a problem except that the casualty in all of this is the brands that we are supposed to serve. Getting over this neurosis is going to be important if we're really going to make the best of the opportunities that ideas afford us.

Another major obstacle is organisational. It is vital to get the right mix of people together and give them the space to get on with it. We've learnt a lot of lessons, most of them the hard way, about who and what adds value to the process of developing ideas. We'll discuss these in depth later but one concept we'll touch on now is the role of the client. At the heart of this is the undeniable truth that the relationship between the client and the communications planning process has to change.

Some clients have already woken up to the importance of communication ideas and if they find they're not getting them from their agencies, they have taken it upon themselves to create them. Unilever and SABMiller are at the leading edge of this process. SABMiller places such great importance on communication ideas and communications planning that they view it as a core competency to be developed by all marketing managers. They've invested heavily in a practical programme to develop three-year communication strategies for all their leading brands in the 60-plus countries they operate in. This is an investment in ideas and people, which is a clear statement of belief in the power of ideas to improve their business performance. However, this isn't a complete move away from agencies towards a purely internal function. The SABMiller process involves as many disciplines (and agency individuals) as necessary. The key difference is the level of involvement of the client.

The final obstacle that needs to be overcome is habit. For a long time, ideas have been developed externally, often in secret, and then presented with the flourish of a silver service waiter whisking away the lid to reveal the food. Just think about how weird that is. In almost every aspect of our daily lives, we have moved away from pretension and formalisation: from business clothing and eating out, to the budget airlines that take us to exotic locations for the cost of a round of drinks. Formality and secrecy are one of those habits that we as an industry need to ditch.

The simple reality is that the things that people are most likely to engage with and champion are the things that they have had a hand in creating. A lot of companies have taken their own steps to making this happen and the practice of tissue meetings where half formed ideas can be mulled over under a 'we're not selling, you're not buying' flag is well established. But this interim style isn't enough; the best work is when clients are actively involved as co-creators throughout the process.

The biggest challenge in delivering this is for clients to realise their responsibility, and for some, to adjust their attitude. The vital ingredient in making collaboration work is a mutual respect and an absence of power games. All too often clients act like, well, clients, happy to play the adult role to their squabbling agencies. This imbalance not only reinforces the problem but actually creates it in the first place. Getting to a new level of equality in the client–agency relationship is all important.

There are a lot of challenges to getting this right, but it's worth it. Not only are ideas exciting things to consumers –

they're equally exciting for marketers and the agencies they work with. They make all of our jobs more interesting. We've already said that getting them right is critical for brands but there are also huge personal gains to be made in the satisfaction of working with and creating brilliant communication ideas.

But first, in order to understand the current landscape and exactly what the different types of ideas are, we will have to look backwards. Over time, different types of ideas have evolved and we are now at a point where many different idea types – the old and the new, the inspiring and the exhausted, the relevant and the out-moded – are all jostling for our attention. The ideas landscape is certainly looking fairly messy at the moment and it can be hard to figure out which type of communication idea is right for a brand – particularly for clients, who, after all, are the judge and jury when it comes to assessing their importance.

So now let's retrace the steps of our journey to discover quite how we got to this juncture.

2

The evolution
of magic

ONE OF THE MANY MISCONCEPTIONS ABOUT IDEAS IS
that they arrive fluttering out of the blue sky, like
so many butterflies – beautiful, dazzling and already
fully-formed. But anyone involved in the creative industries
will tell you that a sudden stroke of inspiration – whether it
is for a TVC, a screenplay, an art installation or a song – is a
very rare event. The magic of a great idea is the end product
of a rigorous process. Great ideas require hard work, often
undertaken by many people, frequently over a long period of
time. An idea needs to be carefully incubated, to be nurtured
and fed, to be watched over and protected as it pupates and
spreads its wings, before it soars away and takes on a life of
its own. And just as the creation of ideas can be likened to a
natural process, so the world of ideas can be compared to the
natural world and classified in a similar way. So in order to
understand ideas, it is now our intention to observe how they
have evolved over time and to attempt to classify them into

idea types – or species, if you like – which can be profitably studied. To do this, we have identified four key stages, starting from the end of the Second World War.

Stage 1. Pre-1980. Advertising ideas only

Before the Second World War advertising was barely past the stage of the primordial soup. It was a time when most ads were purely functional and print and radio were the dominant forms of communication. But peacetime ushered in a new era for advertising, just as it did in every other walk of life. And the key catalyst for the extraordinarily rapid evolution of advertising in the second half of the twentieth century was almost certainly TV.

The first TV ad had in fact been aired in 1941 when a TV broadcast of a baseball match was interrupted by the face of a black Bulova watch which ticked through a full minute before fans were allowed to return to the game. It wasn't exactly riveting stuff and the art of TV advertising advanced in leaps and bounds over the next twenty years, particularly as TV sets went straight to the top of every American and European family's 'must have' list.

The 30 second TV spot changed the nature of advertising itself. Advertising became less about informing consumers and more about persuading them through an emotional context. And in doing this, creative directors in agencies soon discovered a way to replicate success and build momentum for a brand. Campaigns were born!

Campaigns are all about creating a device or mechanic that can be used consistently, execution after execution. These devices or mechanics are called advertising ideas. They are what lies behind long-term above-the-line (ATL) campaigns – the golden thread. They allow the viewer to engage more easily with the storyline and get more out of each execution (a bit like watching an ongoing soap on TV). They can be about pretty much anything and we have all witnessed countless iterations of such ideas: a clever thought, a character, a pair of people, a relationship, a funny voice, a specific setting . . . the manifestations are endless. Above all else, they bring consistency to ATL communications, giving the consumer an experiential frame of reference.

But in their early days, they were pretty basic. A 'classic' from the 50s was David Ogilvy's 'The Man In the Hathaway Shirt'. Ogilvy ran through eighteen copy ideas for shirt-maker client Hathaway's inaugural campaign before striking on Baron Wrangell, the man in the eye patch. Hathaway had been producing fine shirts with little real commercial success for 116 years, but with this enigmatic character, Ogilvy provided them with instant story appeal, a concept Ogilvy had learnt from research wizard Harold Rudolph. How, readers wondered, did this dashing fellow lose an eye? An assassination attempt? A bar-room brawl? Suddenly, a Hathaway shirt was not just about its functional benefits: the quality of the stitching or the mother-of-pearl buttons. It was about the emotional benefit of being the kind of guy who would wear one. The shirt was a way of joining an élite club of swaggering, handsome fellows with mysterious eye injuries.

Throughout the 50s and 60s, as creatives hit their stride, the emotional dimension to advertising became more complex and more rewarding. A good example is the UK campaign, 'Happiness Is A Cigar Called Hamlet', which was created by Collett Dickenson Pearce & Partners in 1960. The premise is that a man finds himself in an awkward or embarrassing situation and lights a Hamlet cigar, which helps him smile and forget his troubles. The campaign ran through countless iterations as TV commercials, radio advertisements, print advertising, and on billboards, even spinning off its own book of cartoons. It also turned out to be spectacularly long-running and only came to an end when tobacco advertising was banned in the UK; the adverts were seen for the very last time in British cinemas in October 1999. Indeed, Johann Sebastian Bach's 'Air on the G String', which was used in the commercials, is still frequently associated with the brand today.

1970s ads continued in the same vein, building emotional affinity for products and brands with memorable jingles and slogans that became catchphrases in everyday conversation. Those who lived through the decade in the US still find that certain phrases from the period are burnt into their brains, like 'Bet cha can't eat just one!' for Lays Potato Chips or Orson Welles solemnly promising 'We will sell no wine – before its time' on behalf of Paul Masson Wines. A celebrated campaign for the then revolutionary new disposable lighters spawned 'Flick My Bic', which was adopted as a sexually suggestive phrase and drawled in numerous country and western songs.

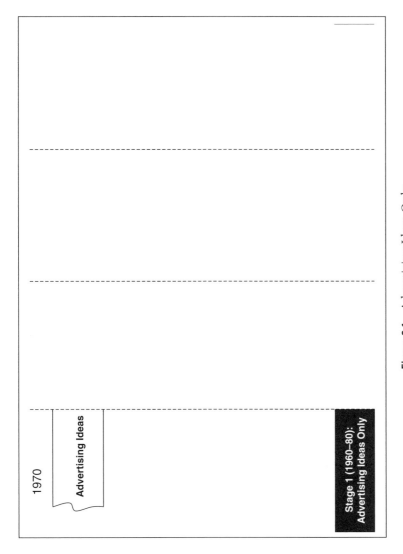

Figure 2.1 Advertising Ideas Only

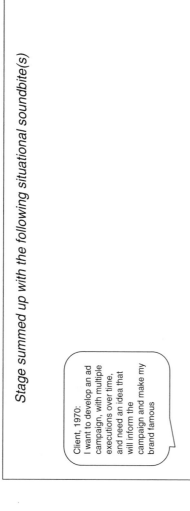

Figure 2.2 Advertising Ideas Only – Situational Soundbites

So during this period, brands were fairly straightforward in their approach to communication. Basically, they went from brief to advertising idea to execution. This approach is summarised in Figures 2.1 and 2.2, first in a time chart and then as a series of sound bites, both of which we will watch evolve and grow as we continue to observe the development of communication ideas.

Stage 2. 1980–1995. Advertising ideas amplified

By the early 80s, advertising ideas were everywhere, and they took every form imaginable. Nescafé Gold Blend ads became famous for the relationship between two neighbours, which developed in soap opera style over a number of years. The Andrex puppy was already busy tangling with its toilet roll and the Duracell Bunny was bouncing for longer than every other toy in the box; and the Man From Del Monte was saying 'Yes!' to swooning fruit farmers.

But the ferocity of competition between advertising ideas created its own challenges and within the increasingly sophisticated walls of full-service ad agencies, strategic planning and media planning started to play far more important roles as providers of added value around the core creative product. Essentially, strategic planners helped creative people to develop more differentiated advertising ideas and media planners helped to amplify them. In this process, media planners probably had the most interesting role, because in looking to amplify advertising ideas, they invented techniques and idea types of their own to help build message relevance and impact.

Media planners did this firstly by exploring the potential of the context – when and where communication occurs. They explored frames of mind, days of the week, times of day, and environment. They started to realise that their job was as much subjective as objective. They started to see beyond the numbers and to understand that how a brand behaved in the world of media could send a subconscious signal to consumers, if the placement was consistent and regular enough. So in the mid to late 80s, they looked at creating consistent media frames of reference, for the advertising idea and its creative expression. The result was that the media property was born! A media property could be anything from the first ad in a cinema reel to the outside back cover of a magazine. The point was for the brand to own a particular space in the media world that it could use as a regular platform for its communications, benefiting from all the associations and expectations that went with it.

And with the development of the media property, media planners started to change the production/media model. Why? Because a media property is fundamentally a marriage between brand and media environment. But as in any marriage, staying in the same place is fine as long as you inject excitement into it. In this case, that meant sacrificing some media money, and repurposing it into production, so ensuring more frequent copy changes. This kind of thinking also laid the groundwork for broadcast sponsorship.

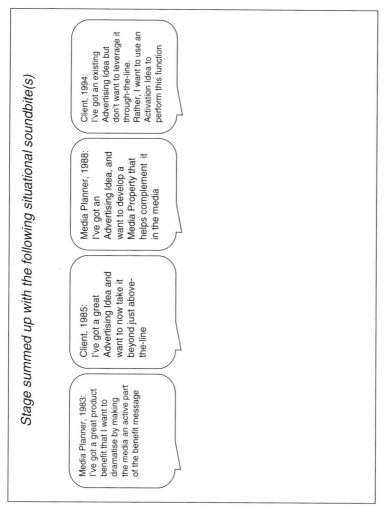

Figure 2.4 Advertising Ideas Amplified – Situational Soundbites

Stage 3. 1995–2002. Through-the-line confusion

So, as we've seen, although change was in the air in the early 90s, advertising ideas were still very important. Renault had great success with the 'Nicole and Papa' TV campaign, which started in 1991 with French teenager, Nicole, borrowing her father's car without permission for a rendezvous with a new boyfriend. Over the next few years, British TV viewers watched, entranced, as Nicole grew into a sophisticated young woman, but still with only one word on her lips: 'Papa'. According to the independent Car Advertising Research Study by Sofres Automotive, the Nicole and Papa story is the most successful car advertisement ever, with a record 93 % recall figure and, more importantly, interviewees could recall that the couple were advertising a Renault Clio. As well as being the best-known car commercial, the British public voted it their favourite car commercial of all time in a Channel 4/Sunday Times poll in 2000.

Even billboards proved that they could still be relevant, with a brilliant long-running campaign by the weekly current affairs magazine The Economist. The campaign used a consistent visual device of white type out of red background, to display snappy and witty phrases, such as 'Great minds like a think', 'I never read The Economist . . . Management Trainee, aged 42' and 'How to win at board games'. The idea behind the campaign subtly flattered the readership by implying that they were brighter, sharper and almost certainly better paid than the average person in the street. And this idea endures to this day.

Figure 2.5   The Economist

But during this period, media fragmentation was continuing apace, and clients were thinking harder than ever before about using disciplines apart from above-the-line. As a result, more and more clients started to consider using activation ideas, as a particularly good way of creating excitement around a launch or as a way of encouraging sampling.

In fact some clients did more than just consider it. Unilever were an interesting early barometer. At this time, they – and the brand consultants advising them – started to look more strategically at how to take brand communication through-the-line. And to kick-start this, they pioneered the concept of through-the-line planning, or communication channel planning, as they called it.

Until this point, they had always enjoyed great success with advertising ideas; many of their local and global brands used them, and not surprisingly, they didn't want to throw all this equity away. So they kept one foot firmly planted in advertising ideas, but the other foot came to rest in the area of activation ideas. They realised that activation ideas could be used through-the-line to drive all communication, including above-the-line. They saw how these could help to achieve multiple communication objectives – long-term brand building as well as short-term sales. And they also saw how they could also rationalise and globalise their brand portfolio, by offering a way for a global brand to do impactful high-production global TV ads at the same time as using activation ideas to bring local relevance and connectivity. And, in focusing on activation ideas, brand-owners like Unilever, and indeed Nike, quickly found the need for something to inform them, so that they retained the brand DNA over time, and did not pull in separate ways but built cumulatively on each other's efforts. To do this, they created what they called activation platforms, which were the first truly strategic type of communication ideas.

But early attempts to find this 'idea behind the idea' were somewhat clumsy. In Unilever's case, they reasoned that these activation platforms should be informed by the brand essence and used for through-the-line execution, while simultaneously using an advertising idea that should be informed by the brand benefit or discriminator, that would be used for above-the-line execution. This caused a lot of confusion for those at the coal-face who were worried that the activation platforms and the advertising ideas might result in very different TV ads.

In fact, most of the initial activation platforms were a specific type of idea that we call physical platforms. These are spring-boards for communication such as music, film, sport, fashion or art.

Nike, for example, developed one around street sport which was used to create activation ideas, such as its 2002 'Scorpion Football'. Axe used the broad area of music and dance. Stella Artois took a media property based on sponsoring upmarket movies and pushed it further upstream, developing 'Movies That Matter' as a physical platform that has endured – just about – to this day.

The inherent difficulty with physical platforms is that they are, by definition, generic. So in order to stake a claim to ownership of them, brands have to invest heavily in defining and communicating a specific point of view with regard to something that is otherwise old fashioned plain vanilla. Plain vanilla simply won't cut it – but vanilla with Valrhona choco-late chunks, infused with acai berries is a different matter! The secret to a successful physical platform therefore lies in transforming the seemingly generic into something unam-biguously ownable. For this reason, Absolut Vodka chose contemporary art – not art in general – as a physical platform. By all accounts, it has proved to be, over years of execution, a successful property for them.

The success of Absolut has led many brands to believe that all they need do is replicate what they have done, but with a different physical platform. However, while Absolut might have managed to build longer-term differentiation for its brand, most brand owners subsequently came to realise the limitations of physical platforms as the drivers of their communication. Many saw that although they were very easy to use, they were strangely uninspiring. They were specific and granular at one level, because they said 'here is a specific physical area like Latin music', but in seeking to drive differentiation they imply a need to 'own' an area, and frankly, any physical area is always going to be too broad to be ownable.

So, physical platforms proved a bit of a disappointment for many clients and agencies and, with a few exceptions, they have pretty much ceased to be used today. Instead, following the logic of brand development from the functional towards the emotional, big clients started to use emotional platforms to inform activation ideas. As the name suggests, emotional platforms leverage emotion above the physical and rational and enable a brand to communicate a proposition or message through an overarching theme that gives the message emotional context and amplification. An emotional platform is usually more engaging and ownable than a physical platform. Nevertheless, emotional platforms are quite broad entities. In fact it could perhaps be said that emotional platforms are not really ideas in the strictest sense, because they lack a twist, or conflict within themselves, to sharpen them up. But the best emotional platforms strike a chord of empathy within consumers and some have the potential to become true social phenomena. A good example is the mobile telephony giant, Vodafone, which historically has built its brand around 'Richer Community Relationships'. And when they are linked to the concrete and specific through activation ideas, they can be effective.

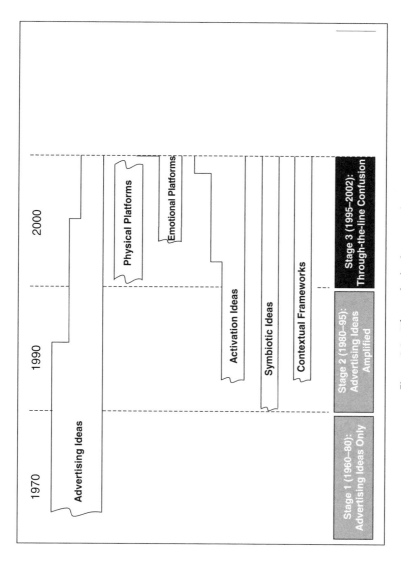

Figure 2.6 Through-the-line Confusion

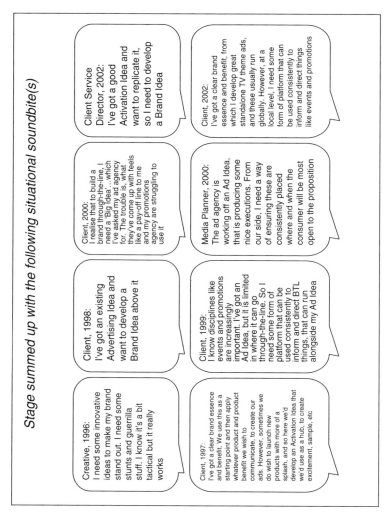

Figure 2.7 Through-the-line Confusion – Situational Soundbites

So, this stage in our history of ideas comes to an end with confusion about how to use both strategic and executional ideas through-the-line. But despite this, a few brand-owner clients and agencies were still looking purposefully for a more simple and effective way of using ideas, as we'll see.

Stage 4. 2002 onwards. Brand ideas rule

The kinds of emotional platform developed during the last stage of our story proved to be the precursor to the optimal type of strategic, through-the-line idea that exists today: what is known as a brand idea. This is a high-level idea which is rooted in the essence of the brand. But whilst this is also true of an emotional platform, that's where the similarity ends. For brand ideas are not as broad and ethereal as emotional platforms. They are more single-minded, focused and directional. They are more down to earth. They are both strategic and creative. And they usually have an inherent point of view. The best go even further, for smouldering within them is an intrinsic conflict that gives the idea energy and makes it very productive to work with. In communications conflict is good. Whether expressed through paradox, contradiction or dissension, communications would do well to adopt greater conflict. It gives rise to energy, passion and enthusiasm. In the words of Carl Jung: 'The greater the contrast the greater the potential. Great energy only comes from a correspondingly great tension of opposites'.

Yet again, Unilever were the most important pioneers. They initially developed this with their global Dove brand, with the brand idea being, 'Real Beauty Is Individual', which they used to build a dialogue and relationship with consumers around the notion of real beauty. At the beginning of 2005, they launched a worldwide project called 'Campaign for Real Beauty'. This featured women whose appearance differed from the stereotypical ideal, and asked viewers to judge them; a woman with a lined face, asking 'Wrinkled? Or Wonderful?' and a young lady with heavy freckles, asking 'Ugly Spots? Or Beauty Spots?' These ads used above-the-line outdoor executions to drive consumers onto the web, to take part in a global debate and to vote on issues relating to beauty – body image and size, age, spots and freckles and so on. They then maintained the momentum using CRM, in-store and table-tops in cafes in an interconnected way to drive home the common message.

Since then the brand idea has evolved further. Dove has recently launched and communicated a Self-Esteem Fund – a fund that supports self-esteem related programmes in countries around the globe. It launched this in the belief that 'Too many girls develop low self-esteem from hang-ups about looks and, consequently, fail to reach their full potential in later life'. And most recently, Dove in Canada launched a 75 second TV ad that dramatises how unreal our ideal image of beauty really is, by showing an ordinary looking girl getting transformed by make-up artists – in fast motion – and ends with the tagline, 'No wonder our perception of beauty is distorted'. The clip has been posted on YouTube and has had a phenomenal viral impact around the world, even to the extent of being featured on a number of TV shows.

So Dove's 'Real Beauty Is Individual' brand idea absolutely has a point of view. It was, in fact, the first Unilever strategic idea to really contain a point of view.

Lagging about a year behind Dove in the development of brand ideas were Unilever's Omo/Persil brand. Up until then, they'd been working off an emotional platform, in the form of 'Modern Parenting' (the view that parents should let their kids experience life and get dirty, in order to develop fully). But around 2003, they found a way to make this more focused and interesting, and reframed 'Modern Parenting' as a brand idea: 'Dirt Is Good'. This is a considerable improvement and neatly demonstrates the difference between emotional platforms and brand ideas.

Other brand owners have also found that emotional platforms could be tweaked to turn them into more interesting, focused brand ideas and in the last couple of years, many clients have started to hunt for these. Some have found them, but many have not, and have settled for something masquerading as one but in reality, usually is just a broad-based emotional platform, or indeed, an advertising idea. Nevertheless, brand ideas have grown in number, as have emotional platforms and the activation ideas which are often used by both of them.

In recent years, advertising ideas have certainly become less glamorous and many people now see through them. They might raise a laugh, and get some awareness and recall for a while, but ultimately they are a bit shallow and don't connect with what people really care about. This has been the case particularly with forward-looking brand-owner clients and in markets that are less reliant on TV.

But advertising ideas are still alive and kicking, just as TV itself is. Take the UK market, for example. Just in the insurance sector, we have seen recent advertising ideas in the shape of:

—More Than and 'Lucky' (a dog)

—Churchill and 'Bulldog' (another dog)

—Elephant.co.uk and 'Elephants'

—eSure and 'Michael Winner/Mouse'

A veritable menagerie, just within insurance! And really, these work well just because they are memorable devices or characters within a relatively boring category, not because they have a really interesting intrinsic idea. So, advertising ideas are still alive, but things are definitely changing. And the only thing holding back an explosion in the number of brand ideas and the activation ideas that express them, is the fact that it is very hard to come up with a good brand idea in the first place.

So this takes us up to today. What next?

Well, if the past experience has told us anything, it's that idea types do evolve to fit their changing surroundings. And for this reason we think another mutation or new type of idea may be just around the corner: what we might term a 'co-brand idea'. This is a brand idea resulting from the fusion of two partner brands' positionings or ideas. It might result from a manufacturer and retailer developing a joint brand idea, from which they then create communication that helps build both brands and businesses. So if we were to take a hypothetical example, looking at Dove's 'Real Beauty' brand idea and the UK retailer Sainsbury's, whose brand idea is 'Try Something New Today'; in this case a co-brand idea would be really interesting, because it'd be a combination of Dove's 'appreciation of how things are' which is the sub-text of their idea, and Sainsbury's desire for 'discovering the new'. The result might be an idea called 'Renewal'.

Now this type of thing hasn't quite happened yet, but things have come close to it, for example with P&G and Wal-Mart, where for the last four years they've run a joint programme in the States called 'Speaking of Women's Health', with educational seminars running in Wal-Mart stores.

An alternative to the manufacturer-retailer source of co-brand ideas, would be with an ingredient brand developing a co-brand idea with its host. Consider a credit or debit card company doing this with a retail bank . . . it might be Visa and Citibank, for example. Or it might be Intel, and a computer manufacturer like Sony.

But in any case, this development will be the result of a more complex business world where collaborative partnerships are on the up and need to use communication as an anchor and driver.

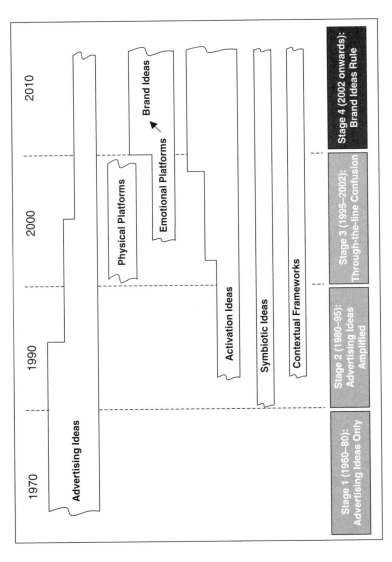

Figure 2.8 Brand Ideas Rule

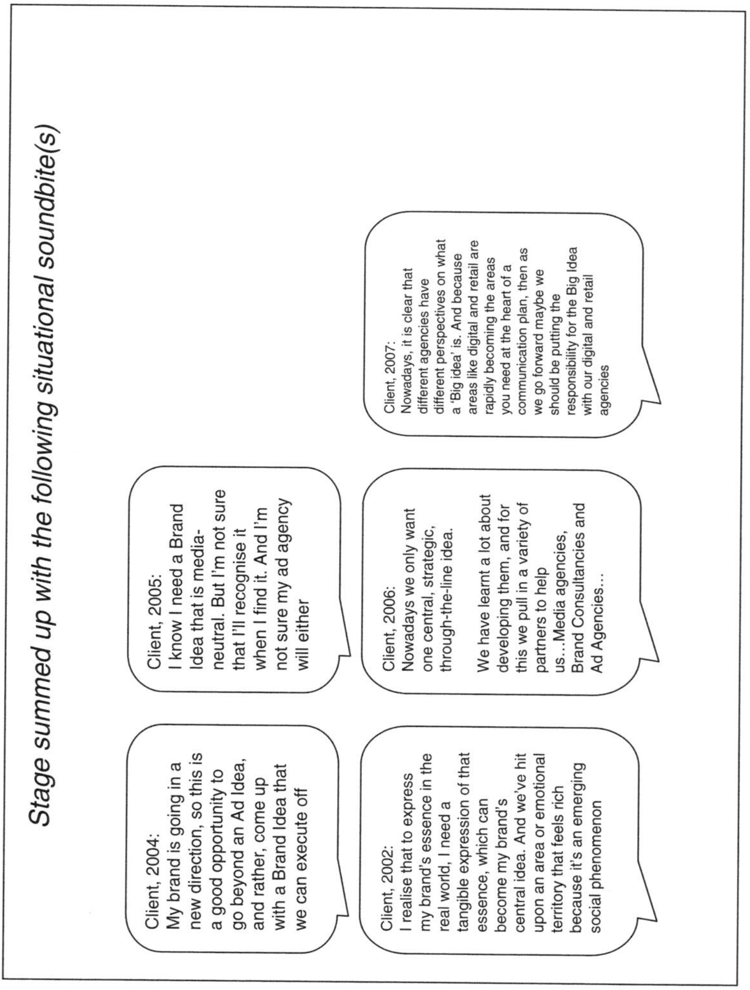

Stage summed up with the following situational soundbite(s)

Client, 2004:
My brand is going in a new direction, so this is a good opportunity to go beyond an Ad Idea, and rather, come up with a Brand Idea that we can execute off

Client, 2002:
I realise that to express my brand's essence in the real world, I need a tangible expression of that essence, which can become my brand's central idea. And we've hit upon an area or emotional territory that feels rich because it's an emerging social phenomenon

Client, 2005:
I know I need a Brand Idea that is media-neutral. But I'm not sure that I'll recognise it when I find it. And I'm not sure my ad agency will either

Client, 2006:
Nowadays we only want one central, strategic, through-the-line idea.

We have learnt a lot about developing them, and for this we pull in a variety of partners to help us... Media agencies, Brand Consultancies and Ad Agencies...

Client, 2007:
Nowadays, it is clear that different agencies have different perspectives on what a 'Big Idea' is. And because areas like digital and retail are rapidly becoming the areas you need at the heart of a communication plan, then as we go forward maybe we should be putting the responsibility for the Big Idea with our digital and retail agencies

Figure 2.9 Brand Ideas Rule – Situational Soundbites

The seven main types of communication idea

In our story of the four stages of ideas, we have identified seven main types of communication idea. These can be summarised very briefly below:

Advertising ideas

These are the ideas that lie behind long-term above-the-line campaigns. For many years, these were at the heart of the industry.

Contextual frameworks

These are frameworks that inform when and where a brand communicates.

Symbiotic ideas

In a symbiotic idea there is some kind of interplay between the message and its media or context which serves to reinforce or enhance the communication.

Activation ideas

These are short-term, exciting through-the-line ideas, often with an event or promotion at their heart.

Physical platforms

These are physical territories for communication such as music, film, sport, fashion or art that resonate with the target audience.

Emotional platforms

These are broad emotional or cultural territories.

Brand ideas

These are ideas based on the brand's point of view on the world.

The three main categories of ideas

We can now group these seven idea types into three main categories, as follows:

Strategic ideas

Strategic ideas live upstream. They are the bedrock of communication consistency over time, with the power to orchestrate communications activity across multiple through-the-line executions. They tend to be enduring and familiar, yet at the same time almost invisible to the consumer. In this category, we would place physical platforms, emotional platforms and brand ideas.

They are not easy to come by. In fact, they are a damn tough nut to crack, even though, when they are discovered it can often seem as if they have been there all along, although perhaps obscured by the cloak of preconceptions and prejudice. But ideas such as these are a galvanising force within an organisation and can become a rallying point for idea generation – a beacon of inspiration if you like, that demands freshness and innovation. They also act externally like a magnet – an energetic force of attraction that brings together brand communications under a collection of uniform experiences.

Executional ideas

These are the Ronseal of ideas: ideas that do exactly what it says on the tin. They inform execution and implementation, and they are easy to express directly through different communication channels and disciplines. They inform the 'what we say', along with 'when and where we say it'. Most executional ideas live independently of a strategic idea, which is not to suggest that they are not informed by a higher order strategic thought – at some level all executional ideas are and the best executional ideas are certainly driven by a strategic idea.

Contextual ideas

These are not ideas in their proper sense, but rather, frameworks for understanding the optimal time when and place where a message should be delivered.

So, we can map out how we see the current communication idea landscape in Figure 2.10 below:

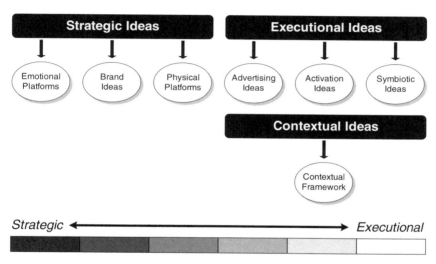

Figure 2.10   The current communication idea landscape

We have seen how the seven main idea types have emerged over time and the categories into which they fit, so now let's move on and look at all these ideas in much greater detail.

3

With an eye
to execution

I'S IMPOSSIBLE TO MAKE A CLEAR-CUT DISTINCTION between executional and strategic ideas. There is always something of the executional in the strategic and something of the strategic in the executional; or at least there should be, if they are to work effectively. However, as we have already seen, some types of idea are more focused on execution and it is these that we will be discussing in this chapter. In the next chapter we'll look at contextual frameworks, and then we'll go on to deal with the more strategic idea types.

As we go, we'll also be assessing each idea type's potential for unleashing energy. A really pure idea is a concept that appeals to both the head and heart. And through this, it creates inherent, latent energy. Not just a little bit . . . but a lot. It has what we call H^2E which can be shown in the following matrix.

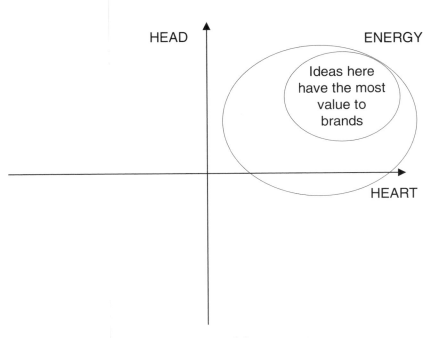

Figure 3.1 Basic Head–heart matrix

So in this chapter, we're going to go through the three key executionally-focused ideas in our order of preference.

Activation ideas

Activation ideas are our personal favourite. In many ways, these are the most important kind of ideas because these are the ones with real, pure energy, which set your pulse racing. Activation ideas are the brand at its most courageous, as if it's decided to throw a party. If the value of advertising ideas is their longevity, then activation ideas should be the brand on its day off. They are the nitrous oxide of communication ideas, they get you to appreciate what the brand is up to in an accelerated way and they are very often what really galvanises both marketing and sales. Just try asking a sales team what's being done to build the brand – and we'd guess that nine times out of ten it'll be an activation idea that comes to their minds first. That's because they bring a sense of ownership and connection that's often absent from other purely marketing-driven ideas.

Activation ideas allow a brand to marry its long term ambition and its long term sense of self with its immediate objectives. They are always about face to face involvement with consumers, always about driving both short term and long term objectives. They enable a global idea to come to life at a local level. Without them, many brand ideas are just good ads, static and with no immediate pitch to get your attention.

One of the other key virtues of activation ideas is that they get people to do something, they get people participating and at their heart they often contain a level of interaction: a promotion, event or some kind of online element. This is where activation ideas differ greatly from stunts which just get you to look at something.

Let's look at four of the most successful and interesting activation ideas of recent years, taken from around the world.

SBAB vs the big four (Sweden, 2001)

SBAB is a Swedish online home loan supplier, competing against the established big four mainstream banks. It positions itself as a small but energetic bank, a consumer champion, that cuts through the red tape by offering low-rate housing loans quickly and simply on the internet. A few years ago, it decided to take its challenge to the big four banks out of the marketing arena and onto the sports field. It created an exciting, memorable activation idea, in the form of a football match between itself and any of the big banks that wanted to accept the challenge. Football was the perfect choice of sport, as it is the 'people's game' and about as far removed from normal banking behaviour as it's possible to get.

SBAB, and TBWA, brought the concept to life with multiple TV ads – initially throwing down the gauntlet, then showing SBAB in training in the run-up to the match, then after the match itself which they lost. But they prepared for every eventuality, and as their CEO said, still in his sweaty football kit, 'They may have beaten us on the pitch, but they'll never beat our loan rates!'

Wilkinson Sword and 'DaRE' (France, 2005)

In 2005, Wilkinson Sword – a brand that had previously not used any specific ideas framework – decided to go to market in France, with an audacious and absolutely brilliant activation idea called 'DaRE', which stood for 'Droit aux Rasages Extravagants'. Sick of Gillette's dominance, fuelled by their belief that the category could be more fun and interesting, and suspecting that people were just a little fed up with the same old ads of David Beckham, they set about creating a series of executions that were a breath of fresh air. How did they do this? By bringing to life the concept of 'the individual's right to shave extravagantly'.

They introduced the concept with an epic TV film, that used narrative, interesting music and visual cues borrowed from fashionable French movies such as 'Amelie' and 'Hidden'. The film plot went like this. Half way through shaving off his beard one morning, a man hears sirens and realises that his apartment block is on fire. So, half-shaved, he rushes outside, managing to rescue a baby en route. As a half-shaved baby-saving hero, he spawns a cult phenomenon of strange, creative facial hair patterns, as well as founding the Association of DaRE. In time, millions of men start to join the Association and shave in strange and amusing ways! After this TV ad (as well as a follow-up version), Wilkinson then ran print ads and drove consumers onto a website, www.dare-wilkinson.com, which both explained the origins of DaRE, as well as having a participatory area where consumers could upload their own funny 'shavings' – and many men did! Besides the general area, a Mister DaRE competition was run which received in the first month, 285 uploaded photos and 400,000 consumers voting on who should win.

Figure 3.2 DaRE Activation Idea

There was a huge amount of buzz and PR around the activation idea. More than 100 blogs relayed the story, 200 forums talked about it and the two films were downloaded and then exchanged around 24,000 times. All in all, it was a huge success for Wilkinson and it showed what could be achieved with a great and original idea at the heart of the communication.

More recently in 2006, and based on the success of the first iteration, Wilkinson Sword have developed a second iteration of DaRE, which they called 'Mask'. This is a parody on a direct-response TV ad, whereby a slick presenter is selling 'the mask' as a way to overcome botched attempts by DaRE engenues to become part of the movement.

Mars and 'Believe' (UK, 2006)

It's funny looking back, because England's football team were absolutely dreadful in the 2006 World Cup. The matches they played in were some of the most tedious in the competition. Nevertheless, if you wound the clock back to the six months before the competition started, you would have witnessed an England full of hope and expectation that this time, they could finally win the World Cup for the first time in 40 years. And this was real hope; it was tangible, it was in the air. Everyone felt it.

This is why Mars were so timely and topical with their 'Believe' activation idea. 'Believe' was all about the Mars Bar as a call to action, driving home the message to consumers to 'believe we can do it'. The beauty of this is that it started on the pack and the pack subsequently became the backbone and domin-ant communication channel of the campaign. By 'pack', we're not just talking about the normal pack with a new tagline on the bottom. Rather, the actual name of 'Mars' was supplanted by 'Believe'. The message took over the Mars bar itself and the name changed for the first time since 1920. So, looking at the 'Believe' bars, the only real links back to the original Mars bars were the colours and typeface of the pack and writing. And also, while the packs might be classified as a 'limited edition' in a technical sense, they were anything but limited edition in a distribution and visibility sense. In virtually every confectionery outlet in the UK, for a couple of months before the World Cup, the 'Believe' bars were visible, either on their own, or, merchandised with the original Mars bars, albeit on a separate shelf to differentiate them. For such a big, mainstream brand with big volumes, this was an audacious move. But it gave the whole activation idea real credibility.

Figure 3.3 Mars Believe No. 1

Figure 3.4   Mars Believe No. 2

Over and above the pack itself, Mars created a theme TV ad that ran intermittently over the month before the competition, together with shorter more tactical spots that ran in the few days prior to, as well as during the early matches.

They also created a website www.marsbelieve.com which was highly interactive. It included elements such as a 'Believe-ometer', a 'Believe Training Ground', which showed how things were aligning around an England victory with humorous examples, e.g. fish and chips in the shape of the World

Cup. It also had a competition element and a place you could 'add a fan' and nominate a friend to their email list.

As well as this, they did a tie-up with the mass, populist daily newspaper, The Sun, and branded their vending machines over the period, with 'show you . . . believe'. At the time, it worked well. It gave Mars cultural relevance, and drove up sales. And obviously since then Mars has reverted to being Mars just as it was before.

Yahoo! and 'Who made the supermodel pregnant?' (Taiwan, 2005)

Here's another great activation idea, this one from 2005, developed and executed by Mediaedge:cia in Taiwan for client Yahoo!. Yahoo! is the biggest portal in Taiwan but Google is perceived as the best search engine. Many internet users will use a Google search even though they set Yahoo! as their home page. In Taiwan, consumers also use searches mainly for everyday information and celebrity/model lifestyle gossip.

So MEC Taiwan created a fantastic idea to encourage the use of Yahoo! as 'the best everyday search engine', by developing a daily online soap opera called 'Who made the supermodel pregnant?'

Initially, they leaked a supermodel pregnancy 'story' to TV and radio stations – Yahoo! wasn't mentioned at this stage. They then launched across TV, press, radio and online pushing users towards Yahoo! Search to become detectives and to find clues. By this time, the media had splashed the scandal across TV, newspaper and magazine headlines and chat rooms. MEC Taiwan fuelled this gossip frenzy with further editorial comment and advertorials.

They then promoted the competition to increase involvement: TV and radio campaigns drove users online to Yahoo! Search. Online prompts stimulated search usage. Weekly print focused on search features and relevant clues. Ongoing PR gave consumers keyword tips, creating the daily information 'fix'.

It was a great piece of activation for the brand, delivering unprecedented levels of awareness and buzz, as well as making an unknown actress famous. And it delivered Yahoo! 1 million unique users, and Yahoo! Search 12 million dedicated searches and over 17,000,000 page views.

Key attributes of activation ideas

- They're short term (but contribute to both long and short term objectives);

- They are content driven;

- They're visible;

- They're about participation;

- They're almost always local (or a local variation);

- They're differentiating;

- They galvanise all brand stakeholders.

Symbiotic ideas

Symbiotic ideas are our second favourite type of idea. You can have a lot of fun creating them and they're rewarding because you can instantly picture them. Symbiotic ideas are all about exploiting the situation or context in which the communication is placed to reinforce its message. They can be a bit like a joke in a Christmas cracker, probably not the best joke you've ever read but somehow the cracker wouldn't be the same without it. But they can also dramatise brand benefits with clever and original interplay between situation and content which genuinely engages and intrigues consumers. Often these ideas are developed by advertising agencies because they write the copy and they're smart at knowing what entertains people (although one claim to fame we have is that Jim won a copywriting award in South Africa for his *Cosmopulliton* ad for Durex condoms – have a guess where it ran?)

Symbiotic ideas are quite polarised in their positioning in terms of head and heart. We've collected together some examples, ranging from those that genuinely create engagement and are strongest in the head–heart department, to those that add little value in the real world.

We'll run through these now, starting with the best first; and then wrap up by showing how they fall on our head–heart matrix.

The Fire Service (New Zealand, 2003)

The Fire Service's 'Speed of Fire' won an award in Cannes 2003. Here, the idea was to dramatise the speed that fire can engulf a building, by using a three minute adbreak to make the point. 'Speed of Fire' commercials ran intermittently with other commercials across the adbreak; each commercial showing how quickly the fire had progressed since the last. It was quite harrowing.

BBC4 (UK, 2006)

BBC4 is a digital channel that's unashamedly highbrow and broadcasts the best of the BBC's cultural programming from documentaries to original dramas to music festivals. Their advertising idea is to present the channel as an island of intellectual depth in a frantic and shallow world, summarised in their strap line, 'Everybody needs a place to think'.

Figure 3.5 BBC4 Bench

As well as a TV promo film they produced plaques for benches placed outside the Royal Festival Hall, London's largest and most varied performing venue. This is a perfect symbiotic idea, not just because benches really are places to think and are filled every day by office workers eating their lunch in quiet contemplation, but the specific location tells you what to expect from the channel. In other words, it is a communications idea as the embodiment of brand experience.

Smart (Germany, 2003)

In Germany, Smart cleverly used the banner of the national newspaper, Der Tagesspiegel, as a communications vehicle by replacing the full stop that was normally in the banner with an image of their car, neatly parked. Again this is more that just a fun piece of execution; it dramatises the benefits of the size and versatility of the car.

Cotibin (Chile, 2005)

Cotibin is a Chilean cold and flu remedy brand, owned by Andromaco. In 2005, the brand created a new and highly innovative media in-store communication with which to express a symbiotic idea.

You know the little ticket dispensing machines that give you a number to tell you where you are in a queue? In-store and in big supermarkets, these are normally at places like the deli or pharmacy. Well, understanding that consumers want instant remedies when they are sick or have a headache, and indeed that brand choice in such circumstances is often made last minute and on impulse – and having the foresight to be able to see an opportunity where none had previously existed – the Mediaedge:cia office in Santiago installed branded ticket dispensing machines at the pharmacy sections in supermarkets and in pharmacies right across Chile. And the message on these machines was perfect: 'Don't wait any longer! Cotibin'. Sales shot up (really, they did!).

Figure 3.6 Cotibin

Yahoo! and Found (UK, 2005)

Occasionally brands dedicate entire campaigns to symbiotic ideas. Tactically these can work very well and perhaps the reason they don't happen that often is that they're actually very hard work! A recent example has been the 'Found' campaign for the internet search engine Yahoo! The idea was that items of everyday life were 'found' by a Yahoo! arrow. This idea relied on multiple executions for credibility and the advertising and media agencies put a lot of effort into placing exactly the right ads in the right places, as can be seen in the example in Figure 3.7 below.

Figure 3.7 Yahoo!

BBC World (USA, 2006)

BBC World in the US use posters that dramatise the notion of seeing both sides of the story. To do this, they have posters

Figure 3.8   BBC World USA

which quite literally go round corners, bending vertically in the middle.

CityLife (South Africa, 2002)

To support its proposition of the entertainment magazine that entertains, CityLife magazine in South Africa used interactive beer mats, whereby you could put your fingers through the holes in the beer mats, and in so doing, add a mischievous element to the pictures. Have a look at Figure 3.9 below, to see what we mean.

Now let's go on to look at probably the weakest types of symbiotic ideas.

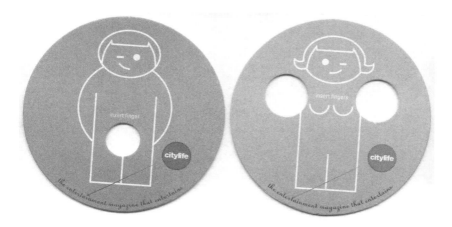

Figure 3.9   Interactive Beer Mats

As we've previously mentioned, broadcast sponsorship can also be a type of symbiotic idea, because it relies on a creative message to build the brand association with the programme. Its effectiveness depends on how creative the brand and its agency have been. Famous Grouse are very creative in their sponsorship of rugby on TV in many markets: for example, in the idents, the grouse becomes a player and fools around or has a cheeky comment or two about the match.

But these sponsorships can often fail because the association between brand and programme is forced and viewers are not required to work to make the connection. In the UK this could be seen in the case of the pharmacy chain Boots which sponsored morning TV throughout one summer, using the slogan: 'Summer on GMTV with Boots . . . bringing you sunshine'. In this case, unfortunately, all the idents were of fundamentally low interest, and all viewers saw was a few people putting on some suntan lotion.

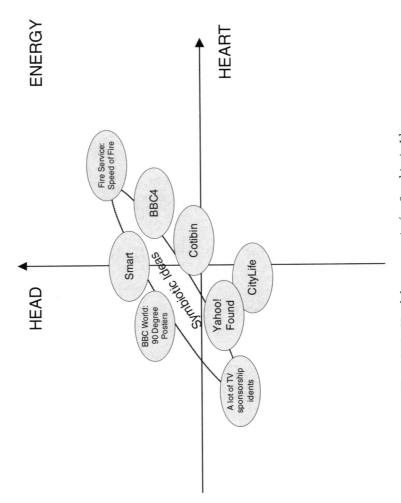

Figure 3.10 Head–heart matrix for Symbiotic Ideas

The trouble with a lot of broadcast sponsorship idents nowadays, is that they are all fairly samey and are in danger of becoming like wallpaper. There are now so many of them, and the five or ten second time length of the ident is so limiting that however hard the agency tries, they mostly come across as slightly humorous, while at worst, downright annoying. In essence broadcast sponsorship is not much more than a cheap way of buying frequency and does not do much to build brand association at all. To express it in terms of our H^2E matrix, we would find the majority of broadcast sponsorships languishing in the bottom left quadrant, which is the one of least value to brands, compared to symbiotic ideas such as the ones used by the BBC and the Fire Service performing considerably better on both measures. This is shown in Figure 3.10.

Key attributes of symbiotic ideas

- They're visible;

- They inform content;

- They involve the interplay of context and content;

- They dramatise brand benefits;

- They're intellectually engaging.

Advertising ideas

Advertising ideas tend to have a natural bent towards and dependence on audio-visual communication. They are often reliant on situational plots and so they very often involve characters: human, superhuman, animal or otherwise. And strangely, this means that they are very often not ideas in the proper sense. After all, you could hardly claim that a straightforward announcement of product features by a talking dog really counts as an idea. Others are more situationally complex and we refer to them in short-hand via the pay-off lines associated with them. Axe, for example, has a situationally complex advertising idea, so we refer to the advertising idea as 'The Axe Effect'. This is fine, but we must be careful not to credit some brands with an advertising idea, when all they really have is a pay-off line. L'Oréal's 'Because you're worth it' is a good case in point. Is this an advertising idea? We don't think so. On close examination, it turns out to be a pay-off line for multiple product ads, with little else really behind it.

When advertising ideas work, they succeed in a habitual and passive sort of way. They play on our need for 'consistency refreshed': that is to say, we all like consistency because it creates familiarity and it helps us understand a brand. So we like consistent characters and we like consistent story mechanics, but only so long as the story itself changes and evolves.

The historic power of advertising ideas – a simple truth well told – can still have an impact as a 30 second TVC, but it should be remembered that these ideas have always had a big advantage over other idea types, as they have always received the lion's share of the investment and, as they are so often repeated, they sometimes get more credit than they deserve.

And, increasingly, brands are finding that advertising ideas lack the stretch needed to drive other forms of communication: branded content, websites, events and so on. After all, how many 30 second commercials could be stretched to make a 30 minute film? They also lack a dimension that encourages consumer participation, which is an ever more important part of a brand's marketing arsenal. Advertising ideas are a bit like starlight – always there, always visible, always giving off light and energy, but at a distance. And these distant stars are also slowly but surely dying.

This is not just an effect of media fragmentation, although that plays a big part. The truth is that a lot of categories are moving into the post TV era already. In most markets, cigarettes are already there and it's easy to imagine the same being true for alcohol and some food categories in the near future. But although they are waning in influence, there are still plenty of brands that thrive on them. People appreciate the entertainment and the little lift that they provide.

So let's look at a few case studies of brands that have been successful with just advertising ideas in recent times.

Citroen C4 and the transforming robot

Since November 2004, when Citroen launched their C4 model, they've used a transforming robot as an ad idea, at a global level. In the first TV commercial, the C4 transformed into a dancing robot that danced in a car park, with choreography from Justin Timberlake's choreographer Marty Kudelka and music from the Les Rythmes Digitales song 'Jacques Your Body'. And when it had finished gyrating, it turned back into the car again. The pay-off line was: 'The new Citroen C4. Alive with technology'.

Not content with one manifestation, the Citroen transforming robot has reappeared, skating across a frozen lake to the tune of 'Walking Away' by The Egg. In making this ad, EuroRSCG hired the British Olympic speed-skating team coach, Nicky Gooch, who skated with electrodes attached to him which were then used to create the movements of the transformed Citroen.

This advertising idea seems to have now gained traction and to have become absorbed into mainstream culture, because recently it's been spoofed by X-Bam (a UK group of CG artists) who showed an old Citroen 2CV trying the same car park choreography as in the first TV ad, ending with disastrous results. The final words: 'Zero Technology'.

Corona and 'Beach in a Bottle'

Grupo Modelo is the Mexican brewing company behind Corona Extra, which is now Mexico's number one export beer. The brand has been a phenomenal success and the communication for the brand has played a big part in this. Rather than competing directly with Bud, in trying to appeal to the testosterone-fuelled American male, Corona has instead built itself around a global advertising idea: 'The Beach in a Bottle'.

This is a very simple idea: what's on offer is the Mexican beach. And actually, at a deeper level, it is also a more laid-back, tropical approach to life. The core ingredients of all the ads that have come off this idea are: the beach, the brand and a relaxed, laid-back mood. So, for example, on TV, there is the one portraying a laid-back beautiful night, with the moon becoming a wedge of lime sinking slowly into the neck of the bottle. There is the one called 'Suitcase', which dramatises the hectic nature of travelling and airports. And then there is 'Prank call' which dramatises the irritations of voice mail – contrasting obviously with the world of Corona.

Print and outdoor ads then play off beach symbolism. For example, there is the execution showing the bottle with a crayfish grabbing it in its claws. Or the one showing a label-less bottle sitting on a beach marked 'Nudist Beach'.

Herbal essences and 'yes, yes, yes!'

We're sure you know this one. You'll have seen it on TV and wondered 'how did they get away with that?' because of the obvious and pretty cringe-worthy sexual innuendo.

Clairol probably don't call their advertising idea 'Yes, yes, yes!' – it's more likely to be 'Female fruity sensual satisfaction' or something like that. But their main form of communication is through TV ads that show beautiful women in showers or under waterfalls in Garden of Eden-type settings in a near orgasmic state because their shampoo is so good. And you really have to laugh when you see the ads.

Our favourite so far has been the one for their Fruit Fusions variant which incorporated talking monkeys (that look like they come from the rainforest) who felt aggrieved because they weren't having as much fun as the orgasmic women. The pay-off line for these ads is 'Totally organic experience' . . . yet more innuendo!

Some of the best of the advertising ideas mentioned here are quite strong in their appeal to both head and heart and so have the ability to create energy for a brand, Others, in our view, are less successful. The head–heart matrix in Figure 3.11 shows our subjective views on the energy-generating potential of some of the advertising ideas we have mentioned so far in the book. Herbal Essences, as you might expect scores far more heavily with heart than head, while The Economist poster campaign, discussed in Chapter 2, is, appropriately, far more weighted to head than heart. The Axe Effect scores pretty well on both measures, although, as we'll see later in the book, it has other communication ideas working for it that might give it an unfair advantage.

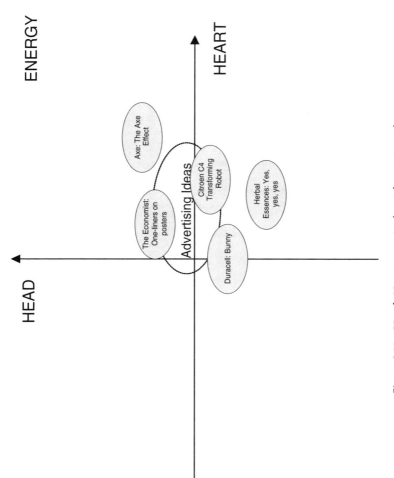

Figure 3.11 Head–Heart matrix for Advertising Ideas

Key attributes of advertising ideas

- They're visible;

- They're enduring;

- They're linear;

- They work through repetition;

- They meet long term objectives.

4

With an eye on the contextual

CONTEXTUAL FRAMEWORKS ARE ABOUT THE 'WHEN' and 'where' of communications. As such, they are really about reinforcement. In many ways they're like radiators that give off heat in a particular place at a particular time; sometimes you might notice that they're there but more often than not, the effect is subconscious.

Contextual frameworks give direction and, when done well, they can add another dimension or spark to a strategy. The key attribute of contextual frameworks is that they don't influence the content; rather, they are more subtle reinforcements of brand benefits or the brand or advertising idea, often working through consistency of placement.

In theory, contextual frameworks should be very useful to all brands. Because they do not influence content, they do not conflict with other types of ideas, so they don't lead to political conflicts between media agencies, who are more likely to generate contextual frameworks, and advertising agencies, who are more likely to have defined a brand idea or an advertising idea. But contextual frameworks should also play a key role in helping brands create more engagement in the marketplace. In effect, they strategically reinforce the consumer's exposure to the brand message when and where they are most open to it – something which is more and more important as consumers become increasingly ambivalent about commercial messaging. And this receptivity can often be heightened when we are communicating a simple brand product benefit.

Here are a few examples of what we mean: When are you most open to a message from a camcorder brand? When you've got a young child who is learning to eat or learning to walk. When are you most open to a message about going on holiday? At the end of a long day at the office or in a grimy depressing subway station. So contextual frameworks help to take us away from simple reach/frequency optimisation planning, towards 'moments' planning.

Because they are subtle, and indeed subconscious from a consumer point of view, we have to assume that contextual frameworks are not particularly strong in either head or heart terms to consumers. Nevertheless, if they serve to make a message more relevant to a consumer, because they are seeing it or hearing it in a particular circumstance or at a particular moment, this amplified effect probably could have either a 'head' or a 'heart' appeal, depending on the message itself.

Media properties

As mentioned earlier, contextual frameworks evolved out of media properties – and in fact media properties are still being used today, as a sub-form of contextual framework. But because media properties came first, let's look at them first.

Media properties are often buying-orientated and are completely about consistency of placement: the first ad in the cinema reel, the first DPS in a magazine, etc. These have no connection to context or brand benefit, nor do they have any real consumer insight driving them; they are more like a piece of real estate that a brand can own. They should do one of two things. They might help build brand differentiation, just by being a good bit of real estate in their own right; but at a far more subtle and subconscious level, they might also convey something about the brand simply because of the consistency of the contextual behaviour.

To understand how they work, think about how we often form opinions of people in everyday life. If you see a particular person in a particular bar at the same time every night, you might well start to form a subconscious opinion of him based on his context (i.e. the bar), as much as what he was wearing at the time or who you saw him talking to. In the same way, seeing an advert for a particular brand on the same page of a magazine every week will also help you to form an opinion of it – in theory anyway! We're not really sure whether it always works exactly like this in practice, especially as media becomes more fragmented, but it's certainly what we in media agencies like to believe. And in some cases, we've no doubt that a media property has really helped to build a brand and there are, indeed, some great examples of the effectiveness of this sub-idea.

In the 90s Boddingtons beer exclusively used the outside back covers of magazines, with a variety of executions all using a visual pun that dramatises their end line 'The Pride of Manchester'. This campaign was very successful in rapidly building awareness of the brand prior to its migration to television. In effect, the idea was to treat the back covers as if they were poster sites. This had nothing to do with the content of the magazines. Of course, to maintain interest the creative work had to be continually refreshed and people began to anticipate each execution, but it was the simple consistency of placement that made the campaign stand out.

BMW is another example of a brand that uses media properties well. They only buy first DPS in magazines which is not just a good position, but also a statement about the car itself. Clinique is another example – they only buy 'Opposite Editor's Page'. In this case, perhaps, Clinique are not just making the brand stand out, they are also ensuring that it is not opposite anything that contains colour or that might distract from its clean art direction.

Conversely, an example where the media property is not as deep is as follows. The major capital cities tend to have landmark poster sites which brands use for visibility and status regardless of the relevance of the content. The two most famous of these sites are Piccadilly Circus in London and Times Square in New York. Both these locations have very long-standing (and expensive) branding from companies such as McDonald's, Coca-Cola and Samsung. These are quite literally media properties bought to give the brands break-out space in internationally recognised (and televised) locations. But the reality of these is that apart from offering stand-out they don't add anything to communications and don't have the depth that a full contextual framework has.

Three key types of contextual framework

Contextual frameworks have evolved out of media properties and are more than about simple placement. They are also applicable through-the-line and not just above-the-line. We have identified three key types:

A. Those that make use of certain circumstances, occasions, particular times and moments (temporal contexts).

B. Those that use environments and activities: these are much more action-focused and often linked to places (physical contexts).

C. Those that use frames of mind and moods (emotional contexts).

Let's look at examples of all three.

A. Circumstances, occasions or particular times and moments (temporal)

GameBoy Console in the UK understand their target are demanding, highly sociable and mobile men, aged 16–24, who want instant gratification, are easily bored, and regularly travel on public transport. GameBoy saw that it could fulfil a role by offering boredom relief for these consumers, while travelling and so in 2002, they adopted the contextual framework of 'Deliver boredom relief for people on the go'. The resultant media strategy was based on reaching people on the go, by using interior tube and bus panels across all key UK cities, with radio as a core support targeted at key travel times (e.g. the regular daily commute).

B. Environments and activities (physical)

To increase the visibility of the new Lexus, and to stimulate test drives, Lexus developed a contextual framework for the brand which was to be wherever their top-end consumers were, be that in business or in key holiday destinations. The resultant strategy meant cars were placed in distinctive upmarket environments, including hotel lobbies.

C. Frames of mind and moods (emotional)

Guinness in the UK and elsewhere, have used a contextual framework to bring alive their brand benefit of 'Inner strength' at the moment when consumers are most receptive to it. This is summarised as 'Intercept moments when consumers need inner strength' and this has driven such executions as the outdoor billboards that ran in the Dublin City Marathon, positioned towards the end of the race at the point at which runners were likely to hit 'the wall'.

Assessing contextual frameworks

Contextual frameworks should be commonplace and should be good news. But in our experience good ones are quite difficult to find. That's because good contextual frameworks need to be both potent and broad in their application (meaning they can widely define how and which communication vehicles are used). But most contextual frameworks are either one thing or the other and not both. Many are potent and interesting, but too niche; or conversely, they are broad but bland. Let's explore this issue with some imaginary examples of contextual frameworks.

Summer romance

This would imply communicating in environments that were about summer romance, which might be in above-the-line media like print, TV or radio or indeed, at certain types of outdoor event or occasion. So it could work reasonably well through-the-line. It's certainly broad, but its weakness is that it doesn't really get to the core functionality or product benefit of whatever category might use it.

Friday night

This would mean putting all the communications into an aperture of Friday night, which is fine as a broad-based buying decision, reaching consumers in a certain time-based window or aperture. Again, it's broad but perhaps not very potent.

Barefoot moments

This might be a contextual framework for a brand trying to link to 'freedom'. But how many times are consumers in a barefoot moment? Not many, so as a contextual framework, it's very difficult to connect to.

Opinion environments

This is about communicating in places where people express opinions. It could be opinion leader columns in newspapers, or letter pages or maybe even outdoor near Speakers' Corner in London's Hyde Park where people traditionally air their views. It's not bad because it's simple but there are only a limited number of such environments, so it would have limited applicability.

Grace under mental pressure

There are quite a lot of potentially interesting areas that could be encompassed here. We might advertise around 'grace under pressure' stories in print, we might appear in certain sports that embrace this notion – gymnastics or diving for example – we might appear in game shows like 'Who Wants To Be A Millionaire', or at certain times of year, such as the four shopping days before Christmas or we might appear in specific places like 'waiting places' or departure boards at airports.

Shared family time

This could be a promising media property – reaching the family together on TV early evening on Saturday and Sunday. Or it might spill over through-the-line to places like zoos or forestry walks.

Moments of inner strength

This looks fine until you try to work with it. And when you do, you realise there are only about five places or situations you can connect with it! It's too personal and too narrow.

Help you look as young as you feel

This might express itself outside doctor's surgeries or on over 50s gym courses, or perhaps through stickers on mirrors in changing rooms. It could also work on talk shows, nudist beaches, internet dating sites, as part of a nostalgic film season or on the birthday page of local newspapers.

Flashy, formal night-time occasions

A brand using this contextual framework could be present at certain types of occasions, like film premieres, May Balls, or Masked Balls. You could ensure you're visible in interesting ways at night-time, perhaps by using phosphorescent ink on outdoor. You could also be in the gossip/people sections of magazines like Vogue and Tatler. But, overall, it's a bit limiting, and doesn't really connect to anything interesting (unless just being flashy is enough for a brand!).

Look good, feel good environments

Here are some examples of these: hairdressers; fitness clubs; beauticians (and even opticians), airports, the changing rooms of upmarket clothes shops, in the beauty sections of magazines and in certain magazines in particular – Hola, Shape magazine, and so on. This is broader in its applicability but it feels a bit undifferentiating.

Before you go out

How do you connect to someone before they go out? By SMS at 6pm, maybe. But if you went down this route you'd soon run out of steam, and it would become apparent, quickly, how restrictive this was.

Even if you've got a potent contextual framework which is relatively broad in its application and has a great insight at its heart, the chances are that this breadth will only affect 20 % to 40 % of the communication strategy. Why not 100 %? Is it because there aren't enough connection points to reach the target audience? Or is it rather, because we are nervous about allowing a contextual framework to be so influential? Is it that we are scared to be true to them? We believe that this is the reason. When, as planners, we come to writing the 'media guidelines' we often end up doing a bog-standard media strategy. Because we know we're not going to deliver the weight

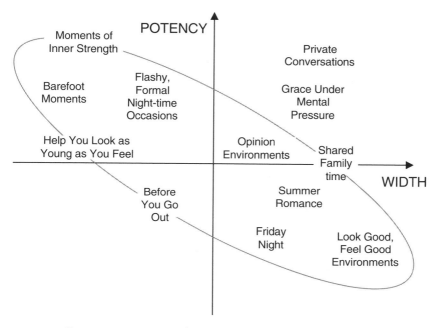

Figure 4.1 Contextual Frameworks – Potency vs Width

that we need off the framework we've got. So, in truth, we still cannot shake off the old ways of thinking, the need for a certain GRP level, and a weight of exposure.

Case study. Domestic violence (UK) and 'Private conversations'

In the UK in December 2003, with Home Office support, a new telephone number and call centre offering help and support to victims of domestic violence was launched. Run by Women's Aid and Refuge, the purpose was to offer victims a simple path to seek help, and rationalise a series of different helpline numbers.

Superficially, the objectives were straightforward – to raise awareness of the new phone number among women and to encourage victims to pick up the phone. Two insights from qualitative research amongst former victims shaped a unique framework:

It's a big step for victims to identify themselves as victims. Communications had to drive empathy and understanding on a one-to-one level, rather than acting as a springboard for a formal public announcement.

'He used to go through everything, so I couldn't even have a piece of paper or an address book'. The controlling nature of abusive relationships dictated the need to be discreet, unseen by the abuser, and offer the opportunity to retain the number for later use.

It is easy to see the tension between the objective of creating awareness and an absolute desire to avoid aggravating an already difficult situation. So it's clear in this case how the context of communications could make a fundamental difference. The contextual framework that was developed was therefore the idea of 'private conversations' – thousands and thousands and thousands of private conversations. These were delivered through:

- the back of shopping receipts, a 'deniable' item;

- partnering the fashion retailer Top Shop and placing posters in women's changing rooms and, again, using the receipts for customer purchases;

- posters on the back of cubicle doors in women's toilets – with special tear-off 'Post-it' notes attached which carried the helpline number;

Figure 4.2 Private Conversations domestic shopping receipt

- radio advertising during coffee time and the afternoon school run when partners were at work;

- women's magazines with PR and concealed advertorials.

Using this powerful contextual framework on a relatively small budget, spontaneous awareness of the single phone line among the core audience of 16–24 C2DE women increased to 33 % from 18 %, pre-rationalisation (dual number).

Figure 4.3 Private Conversations public toilets

Contextual frameworks can sometimes be a bit lame and false, and it's sometimes hard to see where they add value. This idea, on the other hand, has depth as well as a sharp, inspiring thought that adds genuine value without restricting creativity. It also shows that contextual frameworks can come out of insight, which in our experience is a rare thing, as they're often driven only by moments of benefit or consumption.

In many ways, a contextual framework can sound like a sharp strategy statement and for smaller brands they often are the strategy. But for larger brands, it would be rare for the contextual framework to be able to envelop all communications, as the strategy is normally broader, with a contextual framework working as a sub-set.

Contextual frameworks that migrate

Good contextual frameworks also have the habit of changing and evolving and many even start to influence the content. Broad contextual frameworks can often mutate into brand ideas. Imagine as a hypothetical example, a brand that has a contextual framework called 'Mental vibrancy', which means catching people at times when they are mentally highly engaged. Now, it might not take long before you might start doing content around this – starting to create crosswords, perhaps, or Scrabble events. And if this happens, the contextual framework has actually migrated upstream to become a brand idea.

Another example of this – and this time it's a real life example – is from a few years ago, with Diageo's Baileys brand in the UK. Baileys understood that their target derived pleasure from a degree of escapism and 'me time' in the evenings. So in 2002 they adopted the contextual framework of 'Reinvigorate women with 21st Century romance and escapism', and as a result, they started to go into Mills and Boon-type environments, advertising in programmes like 'Ally McBeal' and 'Sex And The City', as well as in the cinema, selecting certain types of film such as 'Moulin Rouge' and 'Chocolat'. But it wasn't long before this contextual framework started to become bigger. Not only did they go on to sponsor 'Sex and The City' but they actually started to evolve the nature of the ads themselves in line with the framework.

Then there is the change that comes about when media properties start to influence content. Here, they don't exactly mutate, but they become symbiotic ideas as well. Take for example, in print, a strip-ad placement on a page three slot every Monday. If you're a regular reader of that paper, chances are that after a few weeks you might notice this regularity of placement and start to associate the brand with this position. But then the brand might start to refer to the context (the editorial environment) in the content of the ads. Now we have something that is half contextual framework, and half symbiotic idea. Or a symbiotic idea that appears in a regular way.

An example of this comes from the late 90s, when Old Mutual in South Africa ran a strip-ad every Monday morning in the Business Report. And every single week the headline changed to reflect the content. It worked so well that in research, we found out that readers actually started to look out for the headlines each week.

Another similar example, from a few years ago, involved Centrum Vitamins. This brand couldn't overtly make claims

Figure 4.4 Old Mutual strip ad

about performance enhancement. So instead, they adopted a media property where the placement of the message was directly affected by the environment. Centrum took a regular front page strip ad in the Monday sports section of UK national newspapers, at a time when separate sports sections had only recently been introduced. Their ad said, 'It's 100%, are you?' which of course would normally fit perfectly with the editorial content of the page which would be reporting on the sporting triumphs of the weekend, with pictures of winning teams, cup winners, celebrating goal scorers and so on. This association with winning was exactly the message that Centrum wanted to get across.

So, contextual frameworks have more to them than meets the eye. They're useful because they add a level of common sense and say 'Don't just trust the numbers, think about what we're actually trying to do'. And in many ways they are a second form of targeting – a contextual target that sits alongside the demographic target – as well as being a bit of common sense that directs the media away from being purely focused on efficiency.

But in many ways, they are also caught between a rock and a hard place. They are constrained by how open we are to applying them in the real world, where we and our clients still care about reach and frequency. And if they're any good, we often find that they are pulled upstream. But none of this should stop us looking for them. Because our view is that good always comes of them; even if it's sometimes just a sharper strategy statement.

Key attributes of contextual frameworks:

- They're invisible;

- They don't direct content;

- They have longevity;

- They support brand benefit (subtly);

- They organise.

5

With an eye to strategy

NOW LET'S LOOK IN MORE DETAIL AT THE THREE IDEA types that have more of an eye towards strategy than execution.

Brand ideas

Brand ideas are the most powerful of all communication ideas. They get people to appreciate a brand, they reinforce what it stands for, they draw consumers in and encourage participation. Brand ideas are inherently flexible and self-sustaining and, like a perpetual motion machine, they don't need external references in order to work. The contradiction they contain should be like flint and steel: strong and capable of sparking huge amounts of energy. They have an aura, a bit like when a person of substance walks into a room and instantly commands respect as a result of their presence and hidden depth. Far from the disposable celebrity of the activation idea, brand ideas are enduring.

Let's now look at three examples of brand ideas which work either with through-the-line activation ideas or go straight to execution.

Rheingold

Rheingold is an American beer that relaunched in 2002. And the really unique thing about Rheingold is its distribution – it's 100 % New York. But in 2003, the New York City government decided to clean up the city. It started with the city's streets and subways, then it banned smoking in bars and even started enforcing the cabaret laws prohibiting dancing in bars that didn't have expensive licences.

Because Rheingold is so dependent on New York, and because the majority of its sales are in on-premise bars whose sales were suffering, the brand felt compelled to fight against this clean-up. It decided to defend what it saw as the true spirit of New York – the 'raw, dirty, up-till-dawn spirit that makes it the most electric and exciting place in the world'.

So, in 2003 Rheingold adopted a brand idea, with 'Take Back New York'. This has become a clarion call, to unite the brand and attack the social regulations that are dampening the city's spirit. With this as a springboard, the brand then developed an activation idea called 'Don't sleep'. In areas where the brand's target ('downtown culture drivers') lived, Rheingold negotiated with local businesses to buy the aluminium night-shades they use to lock up their stores at night. In other words, they used unique outdoor that would only be seen after-hours. And using these 'nightshades' the brand commissioned local artists to paint them with their interpretation of Rheingold and 'Don't sleep'. A second element to this idea was on-premise. In key bars, the brand arranged 'late-night happy hours' from 2–4 am, when the brand would be the cheapest beer. And as a third element, the brand ran TV spots on post-midnight shows like 'Comedy Central', watched by the target between a night out and going to bed.

Since the 'Don't sleep' activation idea, the brand has gone on to do a variety of things, based on the brand idea of 'Take Back New York'. For example, they have sponsored the 'Miss Rheingold' contest. This contest pokes fun at conventional beauty contests; it is only open to bartenders who serve the beer, thereby helping to build relationships with these key individuals.

All in all, 'Take Back New York' is a brand idea that has really connected with New Yorkers. It has created loyalty among drinkers, old and new, and is loved by a lot of bartenders and bar owners.

Camper

Camper is a great example, we think, of a brand that is doing communication right.

It is a relatively small, family-owned shoe brand based in Spain and it has a fantastic and very clear brand idea: 'Walk Don't Run'. It has remained faithful to it for many years. And it activates and executes off it via cool, distinct activation ideas, as well as directly.

In its own right this brand idea is good – it has a point of view on life that goes against the mainstream and is therefore interesting and appealing. But what makes the idea 'sing' is that it is rooted in its Spanish origins: 'camper' means 'peasant' in Catalan and its shoes are based on traditional peasant designs.

The company describes its philosophy like this: 'We have learnt to adapt ourselves to the rhythms of nature and to show the utmost respect for its teachings. To a great extent, this idea explains our way of walking through life. Very close to Earth. With both feet firmly on the ground'.

So how would we describe the idea? It's a Mediterranean cultural declaration that points to the folly of the rest of the developed world. In a way, it's about the race between hare and the tortoise in which the tortoise comes out the winner. It's a point of view that says we need to slow down to make life better. Speed is false economy; being frenetic gets you nowhere (a bit like staying in the office late or pretending to work hard). Technology and modern life are screwing up our heads. Take time for real conversation. Look around yourself. Reflect more. Feed your soul.

The beauty of this brand idea is that it is all the brand really needs. It enables great through-the-line communication, but it also drives activity beyond communication, and even beyond shoes. It is so strong that it is a springboard for anything the company wants to do. It also means the brand doesn't have more idea layers than it needs. It doesn't use platforms of any sort, or advertising ideas, just the brand idea.

Here are several examples of activation ideas that the brand has used over the last ten years:

First, 'The Walking Society'. This is an executional idea that is a bit unfocused in its definition. Nevertheless it has been executed through interesting print ads (often with a Mediterranean feel), through short films, and – distributed in its retail outlets – through ethnic music CDs, and a Spanish–English 'magalog' which is a cross between a catalogue and magazine.

Secondly, 'Shoes & Indigenous Art', a project that invited people from different cultures to decorate Camper shoes. The end result was an exhibition of the shoes that then toured European cities.

Thirdly, 'Walk in Progress'. This was a concept that came about when Camper first went into retail stores directly, and just got off the ground with white walls and shoes on their boxes with no visual trimmings. 'Walk in Progress' was an invitation to consumers to decorate the walls of these Camper shops and express themselves.

Fourthly, 'Casa Camper' and 'FoodBall'. Both are examples of the brand idea brought to life, literally. Casa Camper is a hotel in Barcelona; and FoodBall are cafés that are now in several cities that sell good organic locally sourced food.

Omo/Persil and 'dirt is good'

We've already touched on the subject of Omo/Persil, and its use of strategic communication ideas, a little earlier in the book. But it's now worth going into more detail on this particular brand. Five years ago Jim was a communication planner on Omo in South Africa. At the time, the brand, globally, was using Modern Parenting as their central communication idea. Modern Parenting was (and is) a relatively new approach to parenting, centred on a belief that to grow up, kids have to be allowed to experiment, muck around and yes, even get dirty and that it's a mistake for parents to allow them to cling too tightly to the apron strings. It's a philosophy whose time had come, because kids were (and are) living increasingly sedentary lives, playing with each other less and less, and instead, spending more and more time in front of the computer. As a result, many were getting just a little over-weight. So the idea of Modern Parenting and kids being more active and dirty was something the media had talked about a lot and it was an approach that parents were starting to believe in.

In our terminology, we'd call Modern Parenting the brand's emotional platform, as it's a broad, cultural idea. In any case, it served well enough when Jim was working on the brand, although in some (more dangerous) markets there were cultural issues with it because Mums didn't want to let kids out of their sight; and even in places like Europe and the US, the world had become a lot scarier place for many kids and their parents, than it used to be.

This strategic idea was used to drive a lot of executional ideas, with global and local TV ads being developed, which featured kids getting messy. In South America (where the brand is called Drive), the brand created 'Mancharte' (which translates as 'Get Stained'), which involved events in parks where kids could get messy, doing things like painting or hurtling around adventure playground equipment. In South Africa, the issue was less about dramatising Modern Parenting and more about trying to explain the concept. To this end, an educational programme was developed in the form of a drama series on radio called 'Seeds of Wisdom', that went out every week for about 30 weeks, across nine mass market vernacular radio stations, reaching virtually all the housewives in South Africa every time.

But in more recent years, the brand has taken a great leap forward. The central strategic idea has been given a twist that has given it more attitude and focus. It has gone from something that wouldn't have excited a creative team, to something that now does and will continue to do so. It has become a brand idea called 'Dirt Is Good'. Alongside the new evolved idea, has come a new brand logo, the 'splash', which now features on all products, from washing powder and conditioner, to variants in new product sectors, like washing-up liquid.

It has also energised the executional ideas and given them far more focus. Instead of simply dramatising 'getting dirty', on TV, the TVCs now beautifully depict the motivation, the heroism and fun behind it. So for the ten-year-old boy shinning over the wall to peer at the next door girl, it's not about dirt so much as pre-pubescent love. For the boy fishing with his dad and getting covered in mud, again it's not dirt, but the monster fish that got away. Or for the girl shown on the billboard in the figure below, it's not about the dirty climbing frame that she's playing on in the park, but rather, about her becoming a gold medallist at gymnastics. So the brand idea connects to parents' ambition for kids to fulfil themselves and to the good times parents remember from their own childhoods, too.

The intrinsic point of view of 'Dirt Is Good' has also created more interest in the brand from both the media, and con-

Figure 5.1 Omo

sumers. It's more top of mind to consumers and, as a result, they have proved more willing to reference the brand through its website. So, in many markets the Omo/Persil website has also become more important and consumer-focused and now has a multitude of activity suggestions for parents and kids. In the UK, it does this through a sub-site called 'United Kingdom of Dirt'; as well as with a list of '33 things to do before you're ten'. In Australia, there is a 'Dirt Is Good' club where kids can sign up and get an email newsletter and invitations to events.

'Dirt Is Good' is a great example of a brand idea. It is interesting to consumers. It has a directness and tangibility about it. The only down-side is perhaps its longevity. How do you evolve the idea and layer it over time? But that's a small criticism and the fact is, it's a fun big brand idea that really does have through-the-line executional ideas just dripping from it.

Key attributes of brand ideas

- They're engaging;

- They're long term;

- They can be visible or invisible;

- They organise communications;

- They inspire creativity.

Physical platforms

When a brand finds a physical platform which has a clear connection with the brand or its target audience, it can be a powerful and enduring way to connect, by building appreciation among the target audience, reinforcing brand values and encouraging participation.

But physical platforms tend to suffer from being too broad and very rarely tell you what a brand is really about. Intellectually and superficially, platforms like film and music might have instant appeal, but without a point of view to bring them into focus they can collapse under their own weight. We like to think of them as the black holes of marketing, drawing in more and more expenditure without creating any light.

When physical platforms really help to differentiate brands, they have some value, but because of their inherently physical nature they normally appeal more to the head than the heart. So if a brand were to use 'bookstores' for example, consistently over time, as a place with which to build an association, then you could see this differentiating the brand – because it isn't commonplace. But the trouble is, too often this isn't the case. In most categories, all the players crowd around the same type of physical territories: namely, the ones that connect to their target (their passion) and a usage occasion. In the world of beer and spirits, for example, almost everyone sponsors music. From a consumer point of view it can all become a bit of a 'brand blur'.

However, there are brands which still successfully use physical platforms, but in a differentiated way, so let's look at a couple of examples.

Carling and live music

In the UK, Carling is one beer brand that has enjoyed considerable success in its use of music as a physical platform. It's worth noting, though, that Carling have been smart in having a level of granularity – not just music but live music. This is a particular point of view that stops the idea being too flabby and vague. They started sponsoring live music events across the UK in 1998 and have built up their programme very subtly ever since until in 2006 they had become the biggest single investor in live music in the UK with a commitment of $13 million a year.

In 2003 they started partnering the Academy Music Group which owns some of the trendiest and most prestigious music venues in major British cities. The deal gave them naming rights, so that venues such as the legendary Brixton Academy became the Carling Academy Brixton – as well as the not inconsiderable pouring rights at all venues. But Carling have also staged their own music events, such as Carling Homecoming which took big bands back to the places where they had started out, Carling Live – a series of one-off gigs – and Carling Live 24, a complete day and night of live music at different venues over 24 hours.

The Carling Live 24 events in London in April 2006 featured 19 bands playing concerts in relay at eight venues across the city over 24 hours. So fans would attend a concert by the Kaiser Chiefs at the Carling Brixton Academy in south London, then go out into the street where they would be ferried in Carling-branded coaches, limos and taxis to north London for the next show – Ian Brown playing at the Carling Academy, Islington – and so on.

Figure 5.2   Carling busking on the London Underground

Carling also sponsors two giant rock festivals at Reading and Leeds, but, crucially, they have been very careful not to neglect live music at a grass roots level. One of their most interesting and innovative moves has been to sponsor busking on the London Underground. Until 2001, busking although widely practised on the tube was actually illegal. But when this law was changed Carling spotted an opportunity and worked with Viacom Outdoor to arrange the Carling Live Underground Music scheme. The buskers, who must be licensed, perform on semi-circular Carling-branded mats at busy points at tube interchanges – literally a physical platform both for the live musician and the brand!

The scheme has been very popular with the public who are now guaranteed a higher quality of music than they had in pre-licensed days and gives the brand considerable exposure, as three million people use the system every day. It also associates Carling with real struggling grass roots musicians and the occasional good luck story, too – as several of them have been spotted by music companies and offered recording deals.

Stella Artois and the movies

Another good example is Stella Artois' long-standing association with upmarket movies, which it nurtures by sponsoring a wide range of film-related activities and events. For many years they have been the main sponsors of numerous film festivals around the world and they have also sponsored many movies and film review shows on TV, as well as running competitions to identify and help young film-makers. But they have also innovated in many different ways such as pioneering the outdoor screening of movies in Europe and also showing classic movies in unexpected (but appropriate) locations. So, for example, in 2003, they sponsored a screening of 'Bonnie and Clyde' at a disused bank in Cardiff, Wales and a screening of the Beatles movie, 'Backbeat', at Abbey Road studios in London.

The association of Stella Artois and a popular but highly respected art form resonates well with its UK positioning as a sophisticated 'reassuringly expensive' beer. It also makes a neat fit with its above-the line-activities, as its advertising has become famous for its distinctive style of imitating classic European movies. These began in the 1990s with a pastiche of 'Jean de Florette' and have included ice skating priests, silent comedy and even surrealism for which the slogan was changed to 'Reassuringly Elephants'!

Key attributes of physical platforms

- They're visible;

- They encourage participation;

- They're enduring;

- They're refreshed by new content.

Emotional platforms

Emotional platforms come last in our survey because they are our least favourite type of idea. They are an attempt by a brand to associate itself with an emotional or social issue to give its messages context and amplify its communications. These are the broadest type of strategic ideas, but unfortunately they are often little more than glorified brand essences.

They can work for some brands, but too often they lack an angle, a contradiction, or a point of view to make them really exciting and strong, and so on the whole they appeal more to the head than the heart.

Few established brands have been able to build a successful emotional platform, but let's look at a couple of brands which have tried.

Innocent drinks

Innocent Drinks, the British manufacturer of smoothie drinks is an example of a brand built on an emotional platform – one that is expressed in the name itself. The company was started by three idealistic college friends. They claim that their aim is 'to leave things a little bit better than they found them', which they do by selling healthy drinks made of 100 % natural products. The ingredients are all ethically procured, the packaging is ecologically sound, the carbon footprint is monitored across all business systems and 10 % of the profits go to charity.

This 'innocence' is expressed in all their communications which exude a playful sense of fun across all consumer touchpoints. Their vehicles are painted to look like cows, complete with horns and tails – and they even go 'moo'! The packaging is simple and rather muted, with a clear bottle that uses one colour, which makes it stand out on the shelf as being very different from the other colourful beverages clamouring for attention. Look at the underside of the bottle and you'll see little innocent thoughts, like 'stop looking at my bum'. Even the ingredients list on the side may contain a few surprises. For example, you might be puzzled to read the words 'a few small pebbles' among the list of exotic crushed fruit only to discover at the bottom: 'We lied about the pebbles'.

Their foundation myth also reinforces the same playful, innocent, emotional platform. The story goes that when the three founders were thinking about leaving their regular jobs to start the company, they conducted a little experiment. They bought £ 500 worth of fruit, turned it into smoothies and sold them from a stall at a music festival in London. They put up a big sign which said 'Do you think we should give up our jobs to make these smoothies?' and put out a bin saying 'YES' and a bin saying 'NO'. Then they asked people to vote by putting their empty bottle into the right bin. At the end of the weekend the 'YES' bin was so full that they all went into work next day and resigned.

So far, the company's emotional platform has been very successful – and its secret is probably that it really does reflect the lofty ideals of the company's founders.

Lipton Ice Tea

In Europe, Lipton Ice Tea use 'Spirit of Summer' as their central strategic idea. In our view this is an emotional platform, as the spirit of summer is a fairly broad territory. And to be honest, it shows. Although the idea sounds OK at first, in practice it translates into activation ideas that are generic to the drinks category.

So over the last five years we've witnessed Lipton Ice Tea doing a lot of beach events – such as volleyball, which is shown in Figure 5.3 below – as well as getting involved in music festivals, specifically in the creation of 'chill out T-zones' at the Isle of MTV music festival. In Holland in 2005, to promote the new Green Tea variant, Lipton Ice Tea ran a 'create your own summer' campaign which featured a 24-minute TV ad which was broadcast on the Dutch channel Yorin. But, really, what differentiates any of these activities from something that might be done by Coca-Cola or another CSD brand?

Figure 5.3 Lipton Ice Tea volleyball

Key attributes of emotional platforms

- They're invisible;

- They're long term;

- They can be ill defined.

6

Beyond strategic vs executional

S O WE'RE NOW CLEAR ABOUT THE INHERENT ATTRIBUTES of the seven different idea types, but how do they relate to each other? What are the reference points between each idea? In categorising, we wanted not just to look at the attributes but the relationships between the different idea types across different dimensions. So, we've examined and evaluated the different ideas in the relative dimensions of:

1. The zone

2. Head–heart energy

3. Consumer response

4. Relative energy and longevity

5. Ability to direct activity

6. Visibility

The zone

On paper, a brand expresses itself in loose terms. And so it needs ideas – conceptual entities – to give itself tangibility. But these ideas, in the world of strategic communication at least, should not be too tangible or specific, because they need to be a springboard for execution, rather than the execution itself. Communication ideas can be seen as half-way houses along this route. And they therefore sit in a horizontal 'zone' as can be seen in Figure 6.1 – between vague notions or descriptors (to the left), and specific executional details (to the right).

There is incredible subtlety in this. Change one word in a sentence or idea construct, and its effect is dramatic in terms of where it sits in this horizontal continuum and its potential as a springboard for creativity and execution. Having an intuitive understanding about how vague or specific a notion or idea is, is vital in the game of communication ideas. And here, there is no substitute for intuitive understanding, and, above all else, experience.

So, here's a vague(ish) notion in terms of through-the-line ideation: 'Pleasurable experiences'. Trying to work with this, one instantly realises that there are simply too many types of pleasure and too many types of pleasurable experience. It's too broad and fat. Give it a ten-degree twist. It becomes 'Sensory experiences'. Suddenly it moves to the right. It is

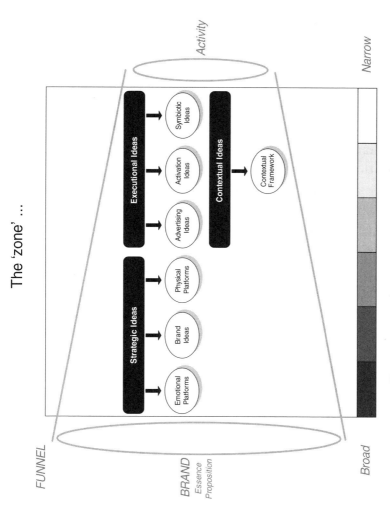

Figure 6.1 Brand essence to execution funnel

quite a lot more defined. Still not great, but certainly more defined. And this is half the skill. Giving things a twist or angle, that bottles interest, energy and tangibility.

Here is another example, but with more subtlety: 'Challenge mindless conformity'. This idea is quite interesting. But it lacks enough tangibility for good, consistent through-the-line execution. And it lacks enough tangibility to give it real energy. What is 'mindless conformity'? You can't wrap your arms around it easily. It's hard to make a list of things that fit neatly underneath it. So it needs a two-degree twist this time. Now it might become 'Question accepted norms and truths'. This is just a little twist – it is essentially the same notion but re-expressed slightly – but 'accepted norms and truths' are entities you could work around more, over time.

Head–heart energy

In Chapter 3, we introduced the notion of the strength of an idea being seen according to its appeal to head and heart, and in fact, the amount of energy it contained. And within advertising idea and symbiotic idea types, we looked at the strength of several individual ideas. But how do the different types of idea interrelate to each other? Let's now go through them.

Emotional platforms are usually pretty broad and worthy. They are absolutely not wrong for a brand, but they just haven't found the angle, the contradiction, or the point of view, that make them really exciting and strong, and reframes the competition. Therefore (as you can see in Figure 6.2) on the whole they appeal to the head, more than the heart.

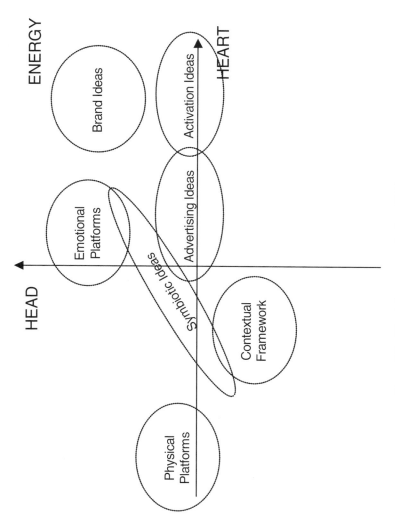

Figure 6.2 Head–heart matrix for all idea types

Once an emotional platform has found the twist or expression that gives it energy, it jumps to the right. It now appeals to the heart as well as the head. It's a brand idea, and it demands activation . . . it oozes executional ideas just waiting to happen.

And the best of the executional ideas will be activation ideas that are pure, unadulterated, and fun. They often appeal to the heart in an overwhelming way . . . much more so than advertising ideas, which work reasonably well, but often only in a habitual and passive sort of way. As we've already seen, some of the best of these advertising ideas – the biggest – are quite strong in both head and heart departments. And others aren't. There is a degree of polarisation. What about contextual frameworks? Well, we have discussed these quite a lot really. They are subtle and are not particularly strong in either head or heart terms to consumers. And symbiotic ideas? Well, symbiotic ideas, like advertising ideas, can also be quite polarised in their positioning. The best of them are really appealing to both head and heart.

And last amongst the idea types are physical platforms, which as you can see in our head–heart matrix are not that impressive. If these helped differentiate brands, they would have some value . . . although because of their inherent physical nature it would be more 'head' than 'heart'. But this isn't the case. As we've already discussed, in most categories all the players crowd around the same type of physical territories; namely, the ones that connect to their target (they're a passion) and a usage occasion.

Consumer response

At a strategic level, there are three dimensions to consumer response.

Appreciation

- How well does the idea create an understanding of what the brand is about for consumers?

- Does the idea type begin to draw them towards the brand in a compelling way?

- What role does the idea play in explaining what the brand is about?

- What is its point of view on the world?

Reinforcement

- How well does the idea reinforce what the brand is about?

- Can the idea build on the brand's foundation of understanding and, brick by brick, construct a distinctive space in consumers' hearts and minds?

Participation

When writing this piece on participation, we were thinking how much it says about how marketing and communications has moved on. If we were writing this ten years ago we're not sure we would have placed the ability to create participation as an equal to the understanding or the continual reinforcement that different ideas bring. But two key changes mean that it is now essential to evaluate ideas against their ability to create participation.

Firstly, this is because our understanding of how decisions are made and attitudes are created has moved on. Now, only the naive would claim that attitude alone drives behaviour. As we have learnt more and more about how the mind works, the AIDA model looks more and more anachronistic.

A – Attention (Awareness): attract the attention of the customer.

I – Interest: raise customer's interest by demonstrating features, advantages and benefits.

D – Desire: convince customers that they want and desire the product or service and that it will satisfy their needs.

A – Action: lead customers towards taking action and/or purchasing.

While actually not a bad guide as to how to write a presentation, this no longer reflects the complexity of most people's experience and many argue that rather than attitude driving behaviour, it is behaviour that drives attitude. In fact, the argument seems to be tipping in favour of the 'I think because

I do' behaviourists. Our suspicion is that these polarised groups will eventually meet on some common ground but, whatever the outcome, the ability for an idea to drive participation is not only valid now but will become more and more important – which brings us to change number two.

Secondly, in Chapter 1 we promised not to rehash the common knowledge about media fragmentation and how it means that communication is getting tougher. However, we would be negligent if we didn't mention how technology is fundamentally changing people's relationships with brands. But far from bringing about the collapse of brand communications, new interactive technologies are now offering more real and more persuasive ways for brands and consumers to come together. 2006 (the year this book was written) probably marked a turning point as the year that the online phenomenon of social networking and shared user-generated content went mainstream. After all that was when News Corp bought MySpace and Google bought YouTube – both companies which were less then five years old but were already valued not in tens but in hundreds of millions of dollars. Irrational exuberance maybe, but what does this tell us about the present as well as the future of communications? Well, if we take Bob Woodward's advice and *follow the money* then the path leads straight to participation.

Both of these changes mean that the ability to inspire or create participation should be a critical factor for evaluating ideas. And in fact at Mediaedge:cia, we believe that participation is so important that we've built our company's offer around it. Hence our proposition: *Active Engagement*.

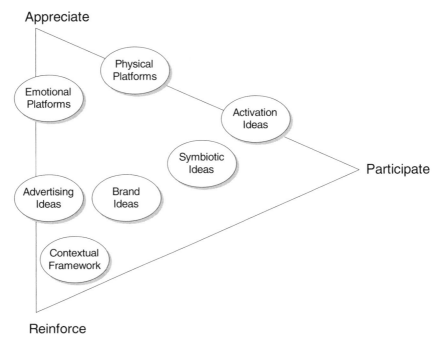

Figure 6.3 Appreciation vs Reinforcement vs Participation

Relative energy and longevity

Out real desire in this chapter was to go beyond the obvious strategic/tactical axis. Unquestionably some ideas are strategic and some tactical or implementational but the tendency is to overvalue the strategic and to be dismissive of the tactical. Let's be clear, however, that they are of equal importance and this equality has never been better expressed than in the Japanese proverb:

Strategy without action is a dream; action without strategy is a nightmare.

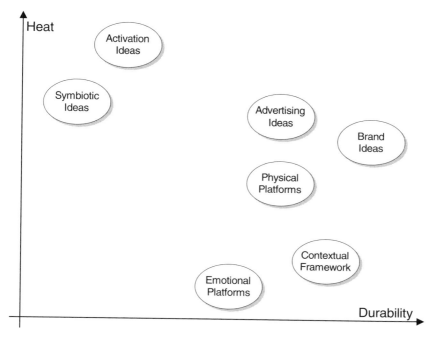

Figure 6.4 Heat vs Durability

A different way of looking at ideas is to look at the axes of heat vs longevity. Heat or energy is something we return to again and again; it is why we create ideas, to give brands the energy to power them forward. Some ideas have more energy than others whereas some last longer. To return to heat analogies, this is a bit like comparing a firework and the sun.

Ability to direct activity

In thinking about the output of communication ideas, we're really looking at two main things – *what* we're going to say and *where* we're going to say it. Different ideas have different influences on these two basic elements.

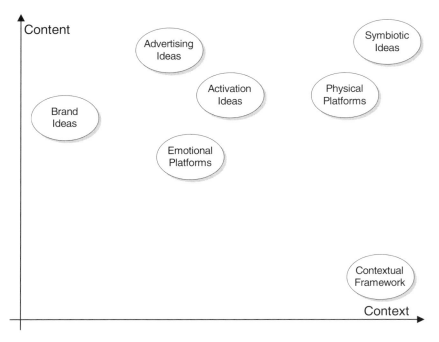

Figure 6.5 Content vs Context

Within 'what we're going to say' it's obvious that while some ideas have a literal role, such as advertising ideas, other have a more subtle role in guiding content (we're really trying to use the word strategic here!). And when it comes to context, this is about geographical placement but it is also broader than that. It also means time, frame of mind and mood; in fact, as we've already discussed, context can be temporal, physical and emotional.

Visibility

Another output is 'what you see' and 'what you don't'. We often hear that good strategy is invisible and maybe this is indeed the case. Certainly, as consumers get better at decoding communications the old syndrome – 'whoops my strategy's showing' – can be fatal for advertising ideas. But not all strategic ideas are invisible, the obvious one being the very nature of physical platforms. Likewise not all executional ideas are visible – we've yet to be in a focus group or immersion where consumers spontaneously talk about a contextual framework but if it's happened to you please do email us.

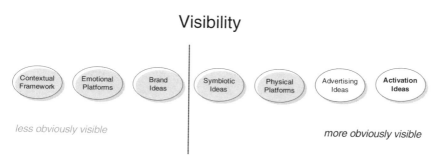

Figure 6.6   Visibility

Conclusion

Communication ideas are strategic and executional but they also have different attributes – abstract attributes like reinforcement, heat and durability and more tangible attributes in the way they effect output, visibility and their longevity. They are just not that simple and the more you examine them, the more differences you see and the more intriguing they become. And we've made clear our sense of the limitations of the strategic/executional axis which we believe is just too shallow. Indeed, to return to Charles Darwin and his worms, dividing ideas rigidly into the strategic and the executional is a bit like Darwin saying:

Ah, yes, the worms. Well, after my extensive research, I can confirm there are in fact exactly two different and distinctive types of worm: the pink ones and the brown ones!

7

Inventing a brand: the 'KR Bar'

A GOOD WAY OF GETTING TO GRIPS WITH THE DIFFER-
ENT types of ideas, is to look at examples of them
all, applied to the same brand . . . in action on the
same brand, if you like.

But rather than try this with an existing brand, we decided
it would be cleaner (and indeed more fun) to do this on a
brand that we've made up. So we decided to create a range of
functional foods for children and in order to capitalise on
an emerging trend, we decided that they should be a range
of functional foods all with omega-3 in them. Obviously
we'd take into account the legislation involved with targeting functional foods at children on a market by market
basis.

Omega-3 is found in fish oil, as well as in things like flaxseed
and rapeseed. Its main claim to fame is that it helps people

concentrate – and it seems this is more than just a claim. In a ground-breaking trial conducted in County Durham in the UK 2005, among 120 school kids, it was found that after three months of taking omega-3 supplements, the kids showed noticeably improved literacy skills, as well as improvements in behaviour and mood.

Think of all the money parents are prepared to spend to help their kids get ahead at school – think of all those private school fees! In a world of ever-more-competitive parents, this is an affordable godsend. Which is why it has become all the rage. But the problem is that omega-3 generally comes either in the form of gooey oil which parents force down their kids with medicine spoons or in the form of massive green capsules. It's just not child-friendly.

So our vision is to create a child-friendly range of foods with omega-3 in them – foods that still taste nice. The only product in the UK that we are aware of, that already exists with this proposition, is St. Ivel 'Advance' milk (which it calls 'clever milk'), and this is being targeted at adults and parents.

However, in our case the plan is to launch a whole range of food products, and target kids directly – in other words, taking the real tough audience head-on (while ensuring we get noticed by their parents, in the slipstream).

By kids, we mean boys and girls between the ages of six and 12, who are at the stage in their lives when memory development is peaking, and when they are developing their own identities fast and hitting what might be called 'behavioural wobbles'. This is also a stage when school is 'hotting up' – when they are starting to come under pressure at school for the first time and find that they really need to concentrate.

> Originally we leapt at the notion of 'Gross Brains' – manufacturing products shaped like disgusting brains – and the extension of this, different types of Gross Brains: dinosaur brains, snake brains, bug brains.
>
> After all, kids love the grotesque, gross and disgusting!
>
> But then it occurred to us that this would only appeal to boys aged four to eight, which might limit the brand, and also we felt that the product was more suited to a slightly older age group.

We have decided to call the brand 'KR' – short for Kids Rule. So our first products would be: the KR Bar (snack), KR Flakes (cereal), and KR Juice (juice) – all to be consumed at the beginning or in the middle of the day.

The time of consumption is designed to tap into the 'omega-3 benefit' and appeal to the heads, hearts and wallets of parents. But that's really where the focus on parents stops. Because the brand that we will be building is one 'by the kids, for the kids'.

Naming this product wasn't that easy. Our working name was 'Memori' for a while, the intention being, to go down a bit of a Japanese/Pokemon type route.

But then we felt we needed a name that would remind parents of the omega-3 ingredient, So one thought was: 'Braino'. Which has a nice ring to it. Another was 'Brooster'... a word formed by fusing Brain and Booster.

But in the end we settled on 'KR' because it locked down the essence and benefit of the brand, to its target audience.

So hopefully you're starting to get a feel for the brand and how it might come alive.

Now for the marketing. We started by creating a brand hierarchy as shown in Figure 7.1.

It's about coming at the benefit discreetly – after all, kids don't want to be 'brain boxes'; there is no direct benefit for them in that. So it's about setting up a situation where they are misunderstood, with ourselves offering a potential solution – as a brand and product range that helps them to get smarter in order to get even with their parents. So if the benefit is about 'getting even' and the essence is 'Kids Made Extraordinary!' and the personality is witty and fun, let's now look, in some detail, at potential communication ideas, going across the three categories sequentially.

BRAND: 'KR' (Kids Rule)
A brand of functional foods, all with omega-3 in them

Target Market
- Primary target is boys and girls aged six to 12; secondary is obviously their parents

Competition:
- The direct competition will be other kids' foods. This includes both food products that parents buy that is vaguely healthy – cereals like Cheerios, Innocent drinks or yoghurts – as well as food that kids buy directly – crisps for example
- However, indirectly, we will be also be competing with more hard-core entities such as:
  - Vitamins
  - The government potentially giving free fish oil supplements to pre-school and primary school children

Brand consumer insight:
- Kids know they're smarter, more grown up and more able than their parents realise

Values and Personality:
We are:
- Macaulay Caulking in 'Home Alone'
- Roald Dahl's books like 'The Twits' and 'James & the Giant Peach'
- Witty, Confident, Funny, Sociable...
- Appealing to both boys and girls

Benefit:
- Get even!

Reasons To Believe:
- Products (with omega-3) that help kids get smarter (as opposed to cleverer) and in so doing, help them get the better of grown-ups
- A Helpline For Kids where kids get advice on how to get the better of grown-ups

Essence:
- Kids Made Extraordinary!

Pay Off Line:
- 'Kids Secret Weapon'

Figure 7.1   KR Bar Brand Hierarchy

Physical platform

First, let's consider strategic ideas. And let's start off by assuming we're looking for a physical platform; so what might it be? Here we need to look to the 'physical' part of the brand – the benefit – for inspiration.

To recap, a physical platform informs and guides a series of activation ideas; it's a territory around physical passions or interests that you can use for your brand on a regular basis as a springboard for activation ideas. And it should be remembered that it's a springboard not a landing point. So if the brand benefit is about 'getting smarter to get even' it's a small leap to being about 'mind and body agility', in which case 'martial arts' could be an option. It's in the right 'zone' – not too broad or fat, nor too narrow. It could make for a series of interesting activation ideas about small guys beating big guys in martial arts tournaments, a bit like in the 'Karate Kid' movies.

But let's assume that a physical platform is not a very interesting springboard from which to build our brand. Functional certainly; but not value adding. So to get to something more interesting and, frankly, something that better represents the heart and soul of the brand, we need to come off the essence: Kids Made Extraordinary!

Emotional platform

Our quest takes us initially to an emotional territory that has an intrinsic cultural agenda. In other words, an emotional platform, in which case 'Kids Think Better' could be an option.

'Kids Think Better' implies a point of view around 'the wisdom of youth' or the fact that kids have purer minds – and that adults have a lot of baggage. But it lacks a bit of humour, attitude and oomph; and it would probably make for relatively worthy execution. So we need to get to a true idea that is more exciting and has a slightly sharper focus.

Brand idea

Our first take on this was 'Grown-ups are stupid' – a humorous take on things, which would lead to executional ideas around how kids could show up and fool grown-ups. But we felt this was slightly limiting. Rather, we'd like to offer up 'If kids ruled the world' as an option. 'If kids ruled the world' drives a real cause for our kids.

Advertising ideas

Let's look next at executional ideas and consider a situation that as a brand we generally execute above-the-line and therefore only want an advertising idea as the foundation for our communication.

If this was the case, for our brand, what would our advertising idea be? Well, as this is a sociable brand, one option would be 'a gang'. A gang is 'kids with kids, adults-excluded' turf. A gang is a consistent set of characters. It would be easy to imagine how we could use this gang as an ongoing mechanic to dramatise the brand and its benefit, using above-the-line media like TV, or a website with interactive games.

But now let's suppose this brand has bigger through-the-line aspirations and wants to come off the brand idea ('If kids ruled the world'), with a series of great activation ideas: what might these be?

Activation ideas

These could be very engaging and great fun. Here are six which would bring to life how kids might rule the world. These might run sequentially over a number of years.

Reverse psychology

The thinking here is as follows. Parents often imagine that they fool their children with reverse psychology. It certainly seems to work if the kid is young enough. Tell a four year old they can't do something and they automatically want to do it! But a six or seven year old is another story, and as this is a brand which helps kids get even, let the kids play reverse psychology on the parents!

The activation might be about kids pretending to be dumb on certain occasions. Or it might be centred on kids creating a secret language where they say the opposite of what they mean. It might even be about teaching kids how to 'throw them a dummy' (an English expression) – getting their parents to think they're about to do one thing, then doing the opposite.

Kids' council

This could take the form of an online election in which a bunch of kids come to rule. These kids could then be used through-the-line to promote the brand.

Kids' newspaper

This would be a real newspaper that would be delivered to kids' houses once a week. It would make sense if this was written by kids. To subscribe, all kids would have to do is register online and enter a promotional code from one of our products.

Kids' laws

This would take the form of a big competition where kids could enter potential laws that they would pass if they were in charge. At the end we'd take the 10 best of them and create a manifesto, as well as a TV ad and poster, for each law.

Challenge your teacher

Over and above these last four 'kids rule' type ideas, we could also include some broader ones of the 'grown-ups are stupid' ilk. So this could be an event at primary schools where 10 year olds get to compete at 'mental dexterity' tests against their teachers. These tests would be the sort that the teachers couldn't revise for!

The stupidest thing my parents ever said

Imagine an online site where kids interact and tell each other 'the stupidest thing my parents ever said' – or the timeframe might be narrowed to 'this weekend'. This could subsequently become a place where kids could upload videos of grown-ups being silly and saying silly things. This might then morph into things like viral content, or AFP content that's shown within kids' TV at the weekend. Or indeed, it could become a source of content for the kids' newspaper.

So as we can see from these activation ideas, the brand idea indeed has some potential. Next up in terms of idea typologies are symbiotic ideas.

Symbiotic ideas

To recap, these are ideas where content and context interplay – creative and media, more often than not. Here are a couple of options for ways they might work to amplify our brand message. First, consider a DPS in a magazine. The proposition is 'magnifies intelligence', but it's written in very small writing on an otherwise white page. However, help is at hand – there is a little magnifying glass to pick up and use to read the print with.

Second, consider a TV ad break, with our brand running two 15 second ads, top and tail. The first ad (the top) would be a statement from a grown-up, a point of view on a topic. The second ad (the tail) would be a kid's point of view on the same topic, but showing much more depth and intelligence.

Contextual frameworks

Here again, there are several fairly straightforward alternatives. If we were targeting kids, an option would be 'Where adults fear to tread'. This would imply kids only environments like: kids' rooms; video games, certain types of TV programme like extreme cartoons. On the other hand, if we were targeting parents, there might be two options: 'Places where Mums gossip' and 'School performance'.

'Places where Mums gossip' plays on the very competitive nature of Mums with kids and the way Mums talk about their kids a lot. The sort of environments coming off this would be quite broad, but could include: cafés in the weekday daytime and school gates.

'School performance' would be more specific and directional. It would be about school league tables (annual supplements in newspapers) but also any content about school exams, or schooling issues.

To remind you of all the ideas we've suggested in this chapter, here is a table of them:

IDEA TYPE	POTENTIAL IDEA
Physical Platform	Martial Arts
Emotional Platform	Kids Think Better
Brand Idea	If Kids Ruled The World
Advertising Idea	A Gang
Activation Ideas	Reverse Psychology
(off the Brand Idea)	Kids' Council
	Kids' Newspaper
	Kids' Laws
	Challenge Your Teacher
	The Stupidest Thing My Parents Ever Said
Symbiotic Ideas	Magnifies Intelligence
	Adults vs Kids POV
Contextual Frameworks	Places Where Mums Gossip
	School Performance

8

Communication combinations

S O FAR WE HAVE SEEN THE IDEA TYPES IN A RELATIVELY pure form. In reality, however, many brands use ideas in a more complex way, combining different types of idea, with strategic ideas being brought to life through executional and contextual ideas. So in this chapter, we are going to explore five ways in which leading brands are currently combining communication ideas, represented by five case studies.

Nike

Nike is a great example of a brand that uses a physical platform in combination with through-the-line activation ideas, as well as using stand-alone above-the-line executions. We admire many things about it, particularly its confidence.

When they create an event, they activate it brilliantly and with massive conviction. When they do a global TV ad, they do it with no-holds barred on the production budgets. 'To succeed with consumers, you have to wake them up', said Phil Knight. But Nike is also interesting for its contradictions.

Firstly, because in direct contradiction of the cult-of-personality that surrounds its multi-million-dollar celebrity endorsements, its communication pretends to strip away the glamorous impedimenta that clutters up modern sport, returning it to the fundamental spirit of competition. Secondly, because it follows an apparently limited and now somewhat old-fashioned model for how it uses communication ideas – but it gets away with it!

In other words, it runs great stand-alone executions – usually global TV ads, but it also uses, as another key pillar of its communication, a physical platform – street sport – which it then brings to life at both a global and local level through activation ideas. It gets away with it, because fundamentally the brand is so well defined already and has a clear positioning both on paper and in the heads of consumers. It also gets away with it because all the activation ideas that come off the physical platform of street sport, are utterly brilliant in their own right.

All the activation ideas are examples of what is called 'Surpetition'. That is, the practice of 'creating your own space instead of competing head-on with competitors'. In other words, it doesn't sponsor existing events. It creates its own, and each one of them is ballsy and original. So let's look at some of them.

Run London (2001 onwards)

Nike first created 'Run London', a 10 km run, in 2001. Since its inception when approximately 10,000 runners took part, it has become an annual event that has grown in popularity, and in 2005 there were approximately 35,000 runners in the main race. In 2006 it's projected there will be 45,000.

What is more, Nike have managed to build off the main event and create an activation idea lasting for at least six months of the year. They have done this through relationship marketing, signing up runners and would-be runners to a training programme with a series of events building to the main one, in effect, weaving the event into the lives of London's running enthusiasts.

In terms of innovation, they do a couple of things very well. Firstly, each year the main event is themed differently – in 2004, it was 'Go Nocturnal' for example, and it took place on the streets of London on the night of November 22nd. In 2005 the theme was 'I will run for a year', so prior to the 2005 main event there was a series of events stretching across virtually a whole year: 'Run November', 'Run January' and so on. Secondly, they build innovative technology into the events. A couple of years back it was the first use of an RFID tag in your shoe that allowed your friends to track your progress in the race, and also meant you could download a picture of yourself crossing the finishing line afterwards. In 2006, there were two pieces of innovation. There was a tie-in with iPod, whereby if you wore a Nike+ shoe you could install a receiver that synchronised with an iPod Nano to record your performance, as

Figure 8.1   Nike Run Warsaw

you ran. Also, by teaming up with Google Maps, Nike created an online 'Routefinder' to help runners find the most appropriate routes for their training needs, as well as to save and share their favourite routes.

And lastly, all that remains to be said about 'Run London' is that Nike use communication in and around the main event extremely well, amplifying it through great TV, innovative use of billboards and buses, all in such a way that it becomes a significant brand statement to millions of people. In fact, the idea has worked so well that it's now been exported to other cities, such as Paris and even Warsaw, as you can see from the picture of the innovative outdoor hoarding shown in Figure 8.1.

Scorpion Football, 2002

At the 2002 World Cup, Adidas was the official sponsor, so Nike created 'Scorpion Football', an activation idea based around the notion of how football is played on the streets, namely, three-a-side, no keeper and first goal wins. Around this core, it created its own tournament – a massive three-a-side soccer competition at landmark locations in 25 cities around the world, where a local team could play against Nike World Cup stars.

It created interest and involvement in the competition locally with street media – using flyposting and phone boxes. But it also created much wider involvement and passion via a global TV spot with the Nike World Cup stars playing in the hull of a ship (and with ex Manchester United and France star, Eric Cantona as the referee); the music and advertising theme tune subsequently went to number one in the charts.

For fans, Nike represented the interesting, dark underbelly of the World Cup, and the real deal. The whole thing had an authentically underground, street feel, in a completely mainstream piece of activity.

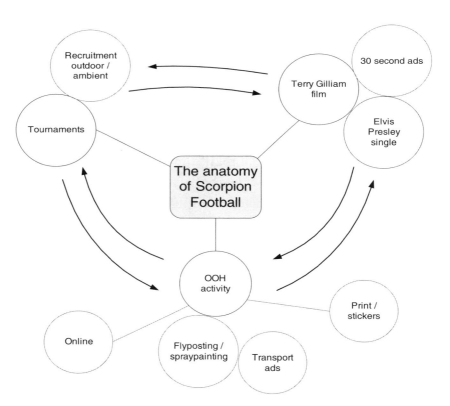

Figure 8.2　The anatomy of Scorpion Football

Freestyle Challenge, 2003

Freestyle Challenge was all about celebrating freestyle, the cross-over between hip-hop music and sport (particularly basketball, but also involving football and even frisbee) which is all about self-expression and 'the moves'.

This activation idea centred on a challenge to find the best freestylers in all three genres. It was executed with local competitions but also amplified through several global TV spots (the best featuring Ronaldinho) as well as through the use of digital, and graffitied Freestyle Challenge logos on the walls of basketball courts.

In the UK, for example, Nike partnered MTV, to launch the Freestyle Face-Off competition. This featured programme slots on MTV which showcased freestylers, and took free-stylers to different places to 'face-off' against each other. It also featured a series of events in cities across the country, with talented youngsters battling it out to get into the 'finals' stage. At the finals, the four potential winners ran their own 'ads' and demonstrated their skills live on MTV. The public were co-opted into voting for and choosing the winner – using both SMS, as well as interactive TV.

Panna, 2004

'Panna' is the Surinamese word for 'humiliation' and is a soccer-style game based around 'nutmegging' your opponent – kicking the ball through his legs. In 2004, Nike took their Panna Knock Out tournament which had previously only run in Holland, and made it international, with players from France,

Spain, UK and Italy all flying out to Holland for the final. MTV subsequently made a documentary about the tournament.

Ginga, 2005

Ginga was another international football activation idea, although lower key than Scorpion Football. The essence of this idea was about celebrating Brazil as the bastion of 'the beautiful game' and underneath this, the rhythm of art and movement.

The main execution was via an ad-funded film, that explored the life of seven real life characters from different areas and social ethnic backgrounds. This film was shown initially at exclusive, invitation-only event screenings in NYC, London, Milan and Tokyo, and later released at film festivals. Alongside this, there were exhibitions by graffiti artists, a CD, some outdoor, a website, and a range of new products called US Gemeos Nike Zoom Air FCs.

Joga Bonito, 2006

Taking the association between Nike and Brazilian football one step further, again going alongside the World Cup and Adidas' sponsorship of it in terms of timing, Nike created 'Joga Bonito' which is the Portuguese expression Pele once used to describe 'the beautiful game'. It was a double-edged dig at Adidas in the sense that it reminded us that the world champion Brazilians (at least prior to the event) are a Nike squad, and that they play much more creative football than Adidas' home team of Germany.

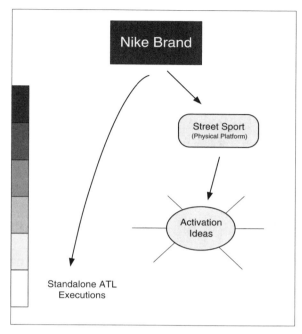

Figure 8.3 Nike Go To Market Model

This was executed with a series of eight lovely TV ads, all urging a return to 'the beautiful game'. Our favourite was one called 'Joy' which featured recent footage of Ronaldinho as an adult juxtaposed with scenes of Ronaldinho as a kid. The soundtrack was all woodwinds and hand claps, and the dusted-off scenes of the child Ronaldinho were lovely to watch.

Over and above this, as with previous activation ideas, there was a strong event element, in this case, a tournament called Joga 3. And, as with the 2002 Scorpion Football idea, this one again centred on a three-a-side competition, aimed at improving and encouraging more skilful play, and teaching young players to express themselves. Nike's new Joga 3 football tournament ran locally, with the national winners going to Brazil for a final.

And lastly, with this activation idea again, a website featured prominently. But in this case Nike teamed up with Google to create the community site www.Joga.com, where football fans could access athletes, chat to fellow fans and participate in blogs on hot topics in football.

Axe

Axe (which is called Lynx in Australia and the UK) is another brand that demonstrates that the brand idea, and the activation off it, is not the only way to be successful. It uses a physical platform in combination with through-the-line activation ideas, and an advertising idea. It is in fact the advertising idea that is the primary driver of Axe's communication, something that could be summarised as 'The Axe Effect'. It's basically a series of demonstrations of the effect of using Axe, with unlikely nerdy guys getting girls swarming all over them. Each demonstration tends to play on a typical male fantasy, which is why guys enjoy the ads so much and they resonate so well.

A typically humorous ad is shown in the illustration in Figure 8.4. You might be forgiven at first glance for thinking this is just a white van. But look again and you can see it's actually a whole series of girls' names and telephone numbers, appearing as if they've been scrawled in the film of dirt on the van side.

But Axe don't just use this idea for ads. Not surprisingly, with the target of young guys in mind, they use it in a variety of

Figure 8.4 Axe Truck

ways – springboarding from a digital platform, as well as creating content that circulates virally. For example, in 2005 in the US they made 'Ravenstoke, Alaska', a short film about what happened to the male residents of a small town when it was sprayed from the air with Axe! Another example comes from Holland, where they created the hilarious 'Essential Scrub Workout' film, featuring 'Stacey Sunshine and her assistant, Michelle', for their Axe Snake Peel shower gels. They also release online video games for PC, such as 'Mojo Master', in which the player had to seduce digital women using Axe products to help.

They also create specific sites. Just in 2005, they created three such sites: firstly, a spoof blog (at www.axe2grind.net) where young men could send in their tales of woe. All had used Axe and all were weary from women constantly chasing them. Secondly, at www.evanandgareth.com, they created a multi-layered blog, starring two young comedians armed with a camcorder and an appetite for making a play at pretty girls. And lastly, at www.Axefeather.com, they created an interactive site inviting viewers to tickle a picture of a scantily-clad woman with a feather-cursor.

Sometimes they also bring the idea to life experientially or through guerrilla activity. Consider the following guerrilla campaign. In South Africa in 2005, to support the Axe Dry variant, an ordinary guy entered a nightclub and was kidnapped by beautiful women. He left behind his bag which was discovered by another group of girls. In the bag were Axe Dry samples, and 'missing' flyers with photos of the guy, above the line 'Have you seen this man? Last seen wearing Axe Dry'.

In Australia recently, they also created a spoof airline called 'Lynx Jet' to launch a new variant called 'Jet'. This began as a brief from client to agency to do some artwork for the outside of a plane. It ended as an activation idea that used TV, radio, DM, web and ambient ideas, including a flight crew of 'mostesses' that wandered Sydney airport, apparently waiting for their next flight to be called. The public was convinced a new airline had actually arrived, and it created massive PR, so much so that the client and agency even looked into launching a genuine airline!

So then why do we call it an advertising idea? Because the idea has, since its inception, been driven by TV ads. It has only gained permission for its non-ATL work, because it has become so well established and so popular through TV.

Consider some of its best TV ads over the last decade: 'Pied Piper', 'Mosquito', 'Click', 'Jennifer Aniston' and the recent 'Billions' (billions of bikini-clad women running through the forests and swimming through the oceans to reach one man).

'The Axe Effect' is one of the most popular, most global advertising ideas on this planet. But, at a lower level of intensity, Axe also use a physical platform in the shape of music and dance. This is primarily as a strategic vehicle which informs on-the-ground activation and sampling, to support the regular new variant launches. Music and dance is a very broad territory and seems a rather obvious way of reaching 18-year-old guys, but at least it gives the brand some sense of where to activate and do experiential communication.

Figure 8.5   Axe Pulse in music store

And in this area they've done many things in many countries, although 2004's Arctic Base Below Zero stands out. This was a 24-hour party at the end of November 2004, in sub-zero temperatures in the Arctic north of Sweden. Three hundred lucky winners of a promotion from around Europe, attended this exclusive party, where they got to chill out with the girls of their dreams, listen to some great bands like 'The Thrills', and participate in things like husky dog sledging, snow-mobiling, ice fishing and even ice dating.

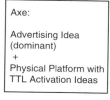

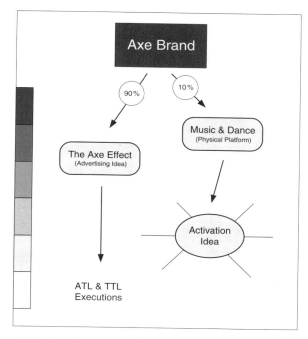

Figure 8.6 Axe Go To Market Model

In 2004, Axe blurred the line between their advertising idea and their physical platform, by launching their Pulse variant in several markets using a classic ad driven by their advertising idea, but then the spot crossed into the turf of music and dance. In South Africa, for example, the brand composed a song, which it then sent to DJ's, as well as choreographed a dance routine, before combining these elements and launching the TV ad. As you can see in Figure 8.5, the brand and variant also had significant presence in music stores.

So in future, maybe they will drop the physical platform and instead use music and dance simply as a reference for content.

Red Bull

In the case of Axe, the advertising idea ('The Axe Effect') is far more dominant than the physical platform ('music and dance') but for Red Bull it's the other way around, with the physical platform being the dominant driver.

Red Bull is a very interesting brand. It clearly incorporates two opposing styles of communication – which fits with the brand and product ethos. This is all about mind and body balance, represented by the two bulls on the brand's logo that, in opposing each other, grow to complement one another. The two styles of communication that Red Bull employs are: the extreme and serious, versus the whimsical and silly. The extreme and serious side is the dominant one and it is what consumers will play back to you about the brand.

Part of this serious side is their use of nightclubs, which is where Red Bull first gained traction worldwide. The brand, at launch in Austria and the countries around it, handed out Red Bulls to club-goers as they left clubs, clearly in need of a lift. And club-goers also soon seized onto Red Bull as a perfect mixer with vodka. Subsequently, in all new markets Red Bull has gone into, the brand has used nightclubs as its initial springboard and trial arena.

Extreme sports, on the other hand, are the true heartland of Red Bull's serious side. Extreme sports are their physical platform. They have become what Red Bull is most known for. They in their own right, are newsworthy and give the brand immense 'energy' and authenticity. So in all key markets

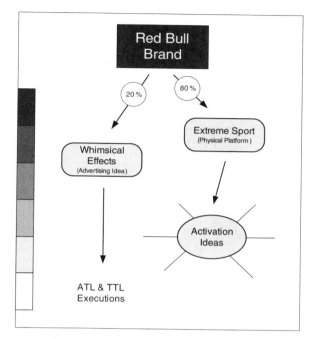

Figure 8.7 Red Bull Go To Market Model

there are multiple extreme sports events every year. There are the bigger ones aimed at the public – air races, street luge, big wave surfing, and motor-racing, for example. Then there are the more discreet events that are aimed at the athletes only – base jumping, for example. These are designed to support a community of athletes and bring credibility to the sports they compete in and often no-one but the athletes themselves know an event is happening.

And then we have the whimsical and silly side. Here, the main modus operandi is an advertising idea that is used globally. To describe this ad idea is simple: it is based on whimsical cartoon animations dramatising the effect of Red

Bull and the wings it gives you. There have probably been over a hundred different TV ads off this same idea around the world, in the last 15 odd years. Here are a couple you might remember. Firstly, there's an old one, featuring Leonardo da Vinci talking in a dodgy Italian accent about 'Red-a Bull-a' and how it 'give you wings'. In this skit da Vinci's insane obsession with Red Bull gets him fired from painting the Sistine Chapel. A more recent execution is about a caterpillar that drinks some Red Bull spilt from a discarded can and turns into a butterfly with the Red Bull logo and colours on its wings.

Bisto

Bisto is a UK gravy brand that has deep roots in UK families. Bisto uses a fairly broad strategic idea territory to inform their communication – which we can surmise to be 'reconnecting families'. This is a fairly good emotional platform for the brand, although it's still pretty broad and it works because it is brought to life by good through-the-line activation ideas.

'Reconnecting families' builds on the heritage of the brand but seeks to re-energise it by connecting to an issue that is highly relevant to today's society: the fact that families don't eat together any more. This lack of family time is seen as a social problem and also has a bad effect on kids who are allowed to eat a lot of junk food, which results in higher levels of obesity. The emotional platform also ties back to the product, and the usage occasion, with food as a form of glue to help reconnect families.

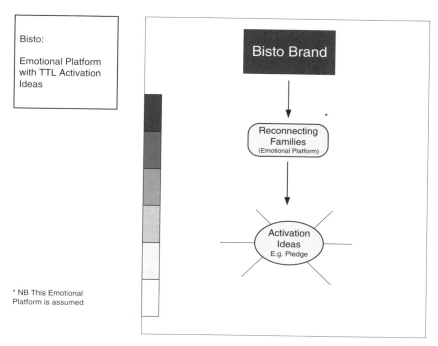

Figure 8.8 Bisto Go To Market Model

To bring this emotional platform to life, Bisto in 2005 came up with 'Pledge' as an activation idea. 'Pledge' was all about championing the family meal, and suggesting that we all pledge to come home on time, for just one night a week, to eat a proper family meal (with a proper gravy!). This night, they call 'Aah! Night'. It centred on a nice TV theme ad, with a series of individuals each synchronised so they talk in turn, to spell out a collective pledge, to get home on time. Running in parallel with the TV was a website where it told you how to create your own 'Aah! Night', as well as letting you download and print off a 'Pledge certificate' for you to sign and place on the fridge door in your kitchen.

We suspect that with 'Reconnecting families' as an emotional platform, there could be many potential activation ideas that the brand could dream up in the coming years.

Yorkie

Yorkie is a UK chocolate bar that uses a brand idea in combination with through-the-line activation ideas. It goes against the grain of the category by targeting men rather than women and, for most people, it is still best known for the 'Yorkie trucker' character in the advertising from the 1980s and 1990s. But after its huge success in those early days, its sales turned flat and its franchise had become blurred to the point where nearly as many women as men were buying the brand.

So in 2002, the brand went into the garage for an overhaul. It came out, courtesy of the marketing team, Interbrand, and JWT, with a spanking new brand idea called 'It's Not For Girls' ('girls' is often considered to be a pejorative expression for women in the UK). This idea takes the macho history of the brand and gives it a contemporary, cultural spin. It takes its cue from the fact that a lot of things that used to be the preserve of males are now shared, and there are very few bastions of British 'male-ness' left. And in the UK, enough had been already done to promote gender equality for people to take this as a joke and realise that the brand couldn't possibly mean it. As a brand idea, it has served well to create humorous, interesting communication over the last few years.

The first thing the brand did with the idea was to create a logo and a piece of point-of-sale – a symbol of a woman with a line through it. They put this right in the middle of the pack itself, in effect using it as a mass-media communication vehicle.

They then did conventional advertising – on TV, print and outdoor. So for example, in the TV ads, we see women attempting to purchase the chunky chocolate bar – but the only way they can do it is by glueing on fake beards, dressing up as builders with hard hats, and swaggering into corner shops asking (in deep, gruff, fake-male voices) for a 'Yorkie please'. In the outdoor, they ran billboard executions such as 'Do not feed the birds' ('birds' being yet another condescending but humorous expression for women) and 'Save your money for driving lessons'. Again poking fun at women, they also created a series of 'Bingo' Beer Mats for guys in pubs that would allow them to 'compare notes' about what their spouses came out with in certain situations. One example – 'Football Bingo' – is shown in Figure 8.9. And on the PR front, Hill & Knowlton

Figure 8.9 Yorkie Beer Mat

sent journalists a list of 'Ten things girls can't do' – such as 'make a decision', 'open a can unaided' and 'understand cricket'.

But since this communication re-launch, there have been many interesting executional expressions through-the-line, too. To us, the best of these and the ones that have demonstrated the true legs of the brand idea through-the-line, have involved both packaging and the product itself. With packaging, for example, they have run several great limited edition/ special occasion packs. One had chunks of chocolate in a pack that looked and functioned like a beer can. Another was on Valentine's Day, and it was a very, very limited edition that

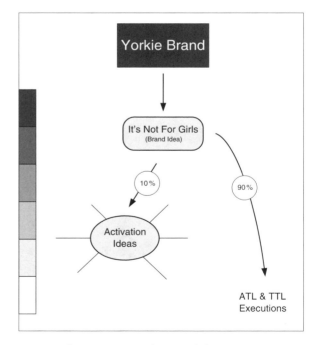

Figure 8.10   Yorkie Go To Market Model

was actually for women rather than men (it was pink rather than the usual blue colour). And another example played yet again on cultural nuance of language, by changing the product name to 'Blokie' (a 'bloke' being slang in the UK for a man).

All very, very brave, if you ask us. But how about this? They also developed chunks of chocolate using the bar itself to play with the brand idea. First, they used the central chocolate block with the 'Not for girls' logo on it; and then they suggested that guys should keep the corner block aside as a 'pacifier' for their girlfriends or spouses!

This is a brand idea with just the right amount of focus. It's culturally interesting. It's simple and non-ambiguous. And it absolutely works through-the-line.

9

Knowing your 'HOCOs'

S O FAR WE HAVE IDENTIFIED THE VARIOUS TYPES OF communication ideas which have been developed and seen how brands have used them. But how do you decide which idea type (or types) will best serve the needs of your brand? We believe that brand ideas are by far the best of all strategic ideas, but they're also the most difficult to create. We have also found that in some cases, brand ideas may not be appropriate for a particular brand or category or even for the culture of the parent company. So it is always worth approaching this stage of the planning process with an open mind. And in this chapter, we're going to look at ways of assessing different idea types in order to decide which one – or ones – will best meet the needs of your brand.

When you're developing ideas they should be objective driven. In the preface we wrote that communication ideas are one of the most powerful ways to drive investment return but (and it's a BIG but) without clear objectives that ladder down from business to marketing to communications your idea is born with an Achilles Heel. Without the discipline that objective setting demands your idea just won't be as robust as it should. This is where the lack of belief in the power of ideas finds itself justified and it's always, always avoidable.

Higher order communication objectives (HOCOs)

Planning is often presented as a linear process, but it rarely turns out that way. This is particularly true in the area of objective setting. We've often seen marketing and communication objectives change dramatically over the course of planning as new insights emerge or tentative executional ideas 'reverse-inform' strategic ideas. In some cases, this is a sign of flexible thinking, but very often it happens because the objectives weren't appropriate for the brand in the first place.

To define the right type of communication idea, you have to start with the right type of objective. More often than not, marketing objectives are not very helpful in creating communication ideas. For example, the marketing objective of increasing the rate of sale by 10 % is perfectly valid, but it doesn't give much sense of what the consumer would see the brand do in the marketplace, nor does it act as a springboard for great communication ideas. So sometimes it's necessary to step back and identify what we call the 'higher order communications objective' for a brand which will then inform which type of idea to look for. We think there are the six key higher order communication objectives (HOCOs), which are as follows:

1. Be top of mind

2. Own values

3. Own a role

4. Reinforce product attributes or benefits

5. Reinforce links to a target market's lifestyle or passions

6. Reinforce links to aperture usage

Each of these higher order communication objectives stakes out a territory for the brand, which should help to tell you what type of communication idea would work best, as well as inspiring execution of that idea and allowing you to gauge consumer reactions. Let's look at them in more detail.

Be top of mind

Top of mind is a place where nearly all brands want to be. (In some niches, there may be some cachet in exclusivity that makes top of mind undesirable, but these are special cases.) There are two main ways in which brands can be top of mind.

Some brands do it through sheer size or scale – the classic example being Coca-Cola. If you walk down a high street or shopping mall in the western world, you're never more than 50 metres from a piece of Coca-Cola messaging: external signage, bar fronts, fridges, umbrellas, etc. This means that Coca-Cola is ubiquitous even before advertising, promotions and brand activation are taken into account.

The second and the most widely practised way of achieving top of mind status is to use a meme or character. These are almost always driven by an advertising idea – the Energizer bunny, the Andrex puppy, the Honey Monster, George the Hoffmeister bear, the Smash Martians, the Churchill dog and so on. This can be so powerful that some of the most famous characters have lost their brand tether and moved into the mainstream of popular culture, such as the red and white Coca-Cola Santa Claus.

It's worth noting that not all of the characters are derived from advertising ideas and occasionally they are driven out of packaging or brand identity, as was the case with the highly successful Felix cat food, although it must be said that even in this example it's the advertising interpretation that breathes life into the character.

Own values

Values are persuasive: they're what draw us to other people. Values, while intangible, are what differentiate us from each other and the 'right' ones (e.g. justice, freedom, fairness) are innately attractive.

Values are often talked about in brand essences. We've often seen them locked away in the centre of brand keys, bullseyes and pyramids and all too regularly that's exactly where they stay, gaining little or no traction in the real world. But when unlocked and directly applied to communications they can be very powerful.

The telecoms giant, Orange, is one of the best examples of owning values. When you look at Orange in all its different incarnations, the underlying value of 'Optimism' (its emotional platform) has more often than not been there, as either the main or secondary message. This is a smart objective for a technology company, as it challenges the standards of the category, presents the brand as human and empathetic and also creates a framework for innovation. The only times when Orange has wobbled are when it has strayed from this core understanding that we all have of its meaning and place in the world. It's a higher order thought that has changed the category and created a territory beyond pure technical innovation for the brand to inhabit.

Own a role

Roles are a more rounded form of values. Less abstract, they are the archetypes of instantly recognisable characters or relationship dynamics, such as leader, wise man, friend, mother and – the most commonly used – challenger.

Roles or archetypes are a powerful shorthand for the relationship you want to create with the consumer and can wire a brand directly into the culture. The author Terry Pratchett has a great perspective on our relationship with stories and the archetypes they contain: 'People think that they shape stories but often it's the other way round.'

This is a powerful thought. The notion that we are shaped by stories makes sense to us, because, after all, our culture is founded on a fairly small number of stories which are simply repeated and reinterpreted again and again.

One of the classic books in this area is *The Hero With A Thousand Faces*, written by Joseph Campbell and published in the 1940s. There's nothing particularly unique about the book, as the stories it contains are as old as antiquity but what Campbell did was to articulate the framework of the archetypal hero's journey:

I.   The story starts with a status quo and we're introduced to our hero in this ordinary world.

II.   He receives a call to adventure and is reluctant at first but is encouraged by a wise old person to cross the threshold.

III.   He encounters obstacles, nemesis and helpers.

IV.   He reaches a low point where he experiences a supreme ordeal, then seizes the elixir or treasure.

V.   He returns home, transformed by the experience, with a treasure to benefit the world.

VI.   The story ends with a new status quo.

We're sure you recognise this story in many interpretations from King Arthur to 'Star Wars'. This isn't whimsy; it's a practical tool that can be used to shape a brand's objectives as there are many stories that can fit the way a brand wants to cast itself. A classic example of an archetype is the Jester. The Jester's goal is to live the moment, have a great time and to lighten up the world. The Jester's role is to be the pin that punctures the pompous, overconfident and arrogant.

It's a classic archetype and casts the brand in a clear role that anyone can relate to. It suits companies with a fun loving ethos and for brands that want to be clearly differentiated from those that take themselves too seriously.

By far the most famous Jester brand in the UK is Virgin. In its most successful guises Virgin acts exactly like the Jester, bringing fun into a category and challenging the status quo created by the arrogant established brands: Virgin Atlantic vs British Airways or Virgin Mobile against those big bullies who make you sign a phone contract. All of the brand's least successful ventures have occurred when it has drifted from this role; when it has been unclear who the brand is lampooning and what Virgin's place is in the narrative.

Owning values and owning roles are both very powerful ways to connect and engage. As types of objectives we believe they will increasingly be the most widely adopted. As HOCOs, they offer the greatest potential for both head and heart appeal and we expect this type of objective to be used more and more as brands look to differentiate, connect and energise. For more in this area, we recommend John Grant's *The Brand Innovation Manifesto*. John has gone into great detail about different roles and types with enough breadth for any brand to cast themselves in their own narrative.

Reinforce product attributes or benefits

Among the many definitions of a brand that are 'out there', the one we feel is the closest to our experience is 'an emotional thought about a rational difference'. And in some market situations simply emphasising the rational difference – the faster, the cleaner, the longer, etc – is the clearest opportunity. While these are often expressed in advertising ideas, some brands and companies have based their strategy on this simple approach.

In recent years, Reckitt Benckiser has shown strong growth within the detergents sector. The company's strategy is to focus on high-powered products in high growth categories. In a cluttered environment, the brands – Cillit Bang and Vanish, among others – have grown rapidly through a single-minded focus on product performance, combined with distinctive, almost garish, packaging and straightforward, straight-talking advertising that borders on parody.

Reinforce links to a target market's lifestyle or passions

As communication ideas moved beyond advertising ideas the first stretch was to find ways of connecting to an audience's passions or lifestyle. These ideas are now well established, but in a lot of cases they don't live up to their potential or are underinvested. As discussed, this has led to some less than optimum models where two ideas run in parallel, sometimes symbiotic, but sometimes schizophrenic. But using a passion or a lifestyle in this way can give a brand distinctiveness and offer multiple opportunities for dialogue.

A great example is the Unilever margarine brand, Flora. Flora has been very successful in building its link with a healthy lifestyle. It is, in fact, a perfect example of a brand in which the dominant idea has become clearer and better defined over time, leading to its present idea of *heart health* which gives the brand breadth as well as relevance. This is more than just reinforcing a product benefit. It's a wider and more engaging canvas that has relevance to everyone and makes great use of marketing assets like the sponsorship of the London Marathon.

Another good example of aligning with a passion is Carling and its sponsorship of live music. As we saw in Chapter 5, this has made the brand more distinctive and has helped propel it to the position of biggest-selling beer brand in the UK.

Reinforce links to aperture usage

You could argue that Carling also fits into this final category – after all, watching live music is a classic drinking occasion, or what we would call 'an aperture'. In establishing a link with an aperture, a brand is looking to improve performance by focusing on or reinforcing consumption or purchase within a particular time of day, day of the week, time of year, or mood, moment, environment or ritual. Some of these occasions are determined by culture with the obvious ones being the national holidays or festivals – Christmas, Easter, New Year, Valentine's Day, etc. But there are also brands which have set their own aperture.

The newspaper brand Metro is a product completely designed around an aperture. This free London newspaper is distributed outside tube stations, on buses and in trains and brilliantly exploits that 20–30 minute commute to work in the morning. When we took the tube two weeks after it launched, we were stunned to see that in a tube carriage of 40 people, more than three quarters were reading Metro and most of those that weren't were reading it over other people's shoulders. This is more than a communication objective, it's a business model, but it demonstrates that if you get the moment right, you can be half way there.

Focusing on the right objective

Deciding on which objective is most appropriate for your brand or market situation depends on the brand's current situation and its ambition for the future. We've produced a list of possible criteria to help you identify the most appropriate HOCO. The list is intended only as a quick guide but by examining the different situations and ambitions we can see which HOCO offers the best potential for established brands or those about to launch.

- Does the brand already carry a certain amount of weight in its category – or does it have the potential to do so?

- Is the category that the brand operates in intangible?

- Is it an impulse purchase?

- Is it a low interest category?

⇒ If your answers are yes to the above, think about using HOCO 1: Be top of mind

- Is the brand looking to change attitudes in the category?

- Is the brand looking to change behaviour in the category?

- Is the brand defending a high market share?

⇒ If your answers are yes to the above, think about using HOCO 2: Own values

- Does the brand have ambition beyond the category?

- Is the category low interest?

- Is the brand looking the reinvent itself?

⇒ If yes, think about HOCO 3: Own a role

- Is the brand benefit more relevant than competitors?

- Does the benefit manifest itself in a social sense (is it 'talkable')?

- Is the brand defending a high share?

- Is it a high involvement category?

- Are you looking to encourage trial?

⇒ If yes, think about HOCO 4: Reinforce product attributes or benefits

- Is the category very cluttered?

- Is it a boring brand?

- Are you looking to bond with core users?

- Does the brand have a lifestyle positioning?

- Are you targeting a homogenous group (e.g. First time mums)?

⇒ If yes, think about HOCO 5: Reinforce links to a target market's lifestyle or passions

- Do you think there's an untapped usage opportunity in the category?

- Does the product have a focused benefit in terms of time of day or day of week?

⇒ If yes, think about HOCO 6: Reinforce links to aperture usage

The HOCOs are starting blocks. As individual areas, they are wide but they help to begin the process of deciding which communication idea offers the best opportunity. We've also been careful not to overly complicate the questions. Most of the questions we ask are simple and would probably be answered in the process of setting out a marketing strategy. However, what we are doing is applying that knowledge and looking at it from the point of view of communications.

Where are you coming from?

To keep things simple, let's imagine that your brand is starting with a clean slate, by which we mean it could be a brand that it is yet to launch or one that doesn't have equity tied up in established ideas or properties. (NB This doesn't necessarily mean brands without any baggage but rather, brands that are looking to change without bringing large amounts of their communication history with them.) So, starting with a clean slate, here's how the HOCOs now correspond to communication ideas:

Starting with a clean slate:

HOCO 1: Be top of Mind?

You need an advertising idea

This is the most straightforward. An advertising idea is the best way of dramatising a brand or product and making it memorable. Other ideas such as contextual frameworks can

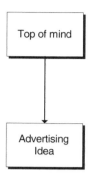

Figure 9.1   HOCO 1 – Top of mind

have their uses but the advertising idea will be at the heart of things.

HOCO 2 and 3: Own a role or own values?

You need an activation idea or a brand idea together with an activation idea

There are two ways of owning a role or values, depending on how well defined the essence of the brand is. If well defined, there is an option of going straight to implementation and the instant energy that an activation idea can bring. This requires some real honesty. This means examining the brand essence not merely as a broad territory that the brand occupies but as a real driver of energising communications. Sadly, almost all brand essences are not up to this application. They can be too wide and flabby to give the communications the edge they need to inspire activity and stick with consumers. However, if you're sure the brand essence is up to it, then go straight ahead.

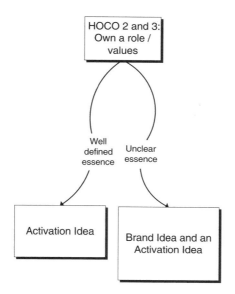

Figure 9.2   HOCO 2 and 3 – Own a role or own values

More often the requirement is for a brand idea. The brand idea provides the stepping stone that opens up the opportunity for the brand to implement in a broader way. From a clear brand idea you can get into the real world and begin some genuinely exciting activation that's sharp and easy to connect with. As we've already seen, a great brand idea coupled with the energy of an activation idea is among the most potent combinations today.

HOCO 4: Reinforce product attributes/benefits?

You need an advertising idea and a symbiotic idea

Clearly defined benefits can be enhanced by the discipline that advertising ideas can achieve, but adding a symbiotic idea can give the benefit considerably more relevance. This sounds

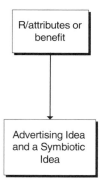

Figure 9.3 HOCO 4 – Reinforce product attributes/benefits

simple but in practice it can often fail to happen because it falls victim to 'not invented here' syndrome. If the symbiotic idea comes from the media agency then often the advertising agency is resistant to changing its creative work; although more often it's the other way round. Advertising agencies can be very good at thinking up great symbiotic ideas and are often frustrated at the lack of engagement from media agencies who put their egos in the way. They fail to make the creative leap from efficiency to effectiveness or just can't be bothered to make the effort to pursue something that's out of the ordinary. This sounds harsh but it's true and all agencies would benefit from more maturity in this area.

HOCO 5: Reinforce links to a target market's lifestyle or passions?

You need a physical platform

Physical platforms are an obvious way to link to a lifestyle or passion. The fact that they're obvious can result in the

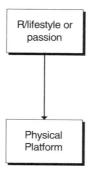

Figure 9.4 HOCO 5 – Reinforce links with TM lifestyle/passions

problems of superficial or low level engagement that we discussed earlier.

However, if you can avoid these pitfalls, a physical platform can bring real rewards in the association of your brand with consumers' passions.

HOCO 6: Reinforce aperture usage?

You need an activation idea and a contextual framework

At a basic level, linking to an aperture is about defining the right contextual framework but to really own and drive behavioural change you should use an activation idea.

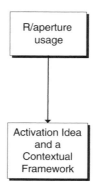

Figure 9.5 HOCO 6 – Reinforce aperture usage

To summarise, here are how the HOCOs relate to the types of communication idea:

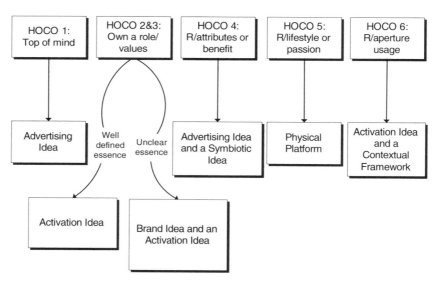

Figure 9.6 When you have a clean slate – Summary

Not starting with a clean slate

So far in this section, we've been looking at working with HOCOs when a brand has a clean slate but if there are exist-

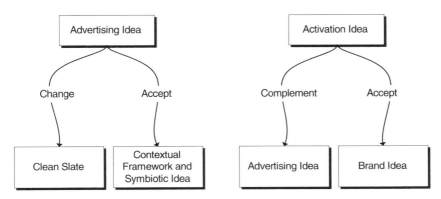

Figure 9.7 When you don't have a clean slate – Summary

ing properties, it can obviously be more complicated and the options will be more limited. In this case, the two existing properties that are worth retaining are normally advertising ideas and activation ideas. If they are genuinely powerful then there will be ways to make them work harder either by increasing their relevance in context and by looking to develop more pure symbiotic ideas, or by isolating what works within an activation idea to see if it can reverse-inform a brand idea.

But the most important factor is . . .

The most important quality required in assessing idea types is good old-fashioned common sense, although it shouldn't be forgotten that this process is closely tied to ambition. Unless you really know what your brand is trying to achieve, any attempt to assess idea types will run aground in confusion and frustration.

10

Generating ideas

ASK ANYONE IN THE INDUSTRY AND WE'RE SURE THEY will agree: the agency world is fundamentally immoral, depraved and debauched and we are all but miserable sinners, doomed to toil away our days in a sea of licentiousness, sensuality and gross materialism. We say: bring it on! But there are two areas where the sinfulness of our industry does cause us grave concern and they are the areas covered by our next two chapters: the generating of ideas and the judging of them.

Huge mistakes are made in these areas all the time. Far too often, ideas – and particularly strategic ideas – are originated at speed by a few people from one agency, sold in a highly competitive environment, and then judged by people who don't have the framework, perspective or experience to do so. All in all, we don't give ideas the room they need and we don't behave as though we respect them enough.

So before we go any further, let's propose and put forward, The Seven Deadly Sins of Origination and The Four Great Vices of Judgement.

The seven deadly sins of origination

- It is a sin for creatives not to be involved in the origination of ideas.

- It is also a sin to leave it entirely up to them.

- It is a sin for those with experience of taking ideas through-the-line not to be involved.

- It is a sin for the client not to be involved.

- It is a sin to originate ideas too quickly and put execution above thinking.

- It is a sin not to get some fresh perspectives from real consumers.

- It is a sin to drift away from the product.

The four great vices of judgement

- It is a vice for the client to be the sole judge of ideas, especially if he or she has no experience and understanding of through-the-line communications planning.

- It is a vice to judge ideas at face value.

- It is a vice to judge ideas by seeing the ATL execution of the idea used TTL.

- It is a vice not to put ideas through a comprehensive road test before agreeing to them.

The sinners

More often than not if a client is looking for strategic ideas they brief an advertising agency. What happens next is that, with some involvement from the account planner, the briefs get passed to the creative department to create the idea itself. All this happens in much the same way that advertising is developed. Occasionally this works, of course, but often it fails and it fails because the ideas are just too ad-centric. They wither outside the linear dramatisation of advertising and typically you only discover this after the event.

This isn't because of a lack of strategic rigour or creativity (in fact, it's still true that advertising agencies have the most creative firepower) it's simply because many advertising agencies have little experience of applying ideas in anything other than advertising. This isn't intended to be provocative; it's a fact.

Do clients brief other types of agencies? Yes. Clients are increasingly turning to brand consultants and the new type of communication independents such as Naked and Michaelides & Bednash. We've got reservations about brand consultancies. At a strategic level they're very strong and they are skilled at developing brand essences and higher order principles, but

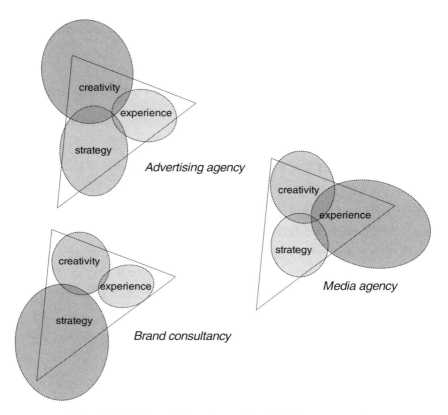

Figure 10.1 The relative strengths of different agencies

when it comes to communication ideas they have the same problem as advertising agencies – they lack experience of implementation; in fact they have an additional problem because they're not as strong creatively.

On the other hand, the communications independents are well placed and are to be respected. They're capable of working in all three key areas – creativity, strategy and judgement – but they lack critical mass and at times look to be straining to maintain the quality of thinking that's given them an advantage historically.

Least often the client will brief the media agency, which is a shame. Media agencies are the most entrepreneurial of all agencies but it's not just this gung ho spirit that's given them confidence. They've found that they're actually quite good at strategic and creative thinking from having the most experience of getting ideas to work in the widest number of combinations.

But ultimately, it's experience that counts. It's only when you have the experience of applying ideas again and again in a combination of disciplines that you get it right. You build up a sixth sense, a crisp quick critical judgement on which ones have real range and depth and which are superficial.

The right mix for the right idea

It's perhaps not a sin, but it is certainly a common mistake to apply the same approach to developing strategic and exe-cutional ideas – using the same people in the same way. Developing communication ideas involves a combination of teams and techniques – the software and hardware of the endeavour, if you like. What's often misunderstood is the balance of the two required for each idea type. All too often the wrong emphasis is placed, particularly with strategic ideas, where too many people get involved and it quickly becomes stifling.

Strategic ideas are best developed with few people and few techniques. The challenge is getting the right people with the right experience and creating the right atmosphere for them to work together. In fact, we don't think that the development of strategic ideas is a process, it's more of an experience, or perhaps we could say that the experience is the process. In some ways we wish it weren't. We wish that you could set a rigid process that guaranteed a hard-as-nails idea at the end of it, but the discovery of such an idea is a genuinely creative event and comes with the discomfort and randomness that typifies any creative venture. We appreciate that this can be disconcerting for clients and that agencies often sell processes for idea generation but the reality is that it is much more qualitative than many people let on, ultimately relying on creativity and judgement.

Executional ideas present a safer area. Their development is more suited to a formal process combining techniques and people to provide stimulus, some of whom may have no experience (what we call a naïve resource). That's not to say that executional ideas don't spontaneously arrive to each and every one of us, it's just that you increase the odds of getting useful ones by taking a more formal approach.

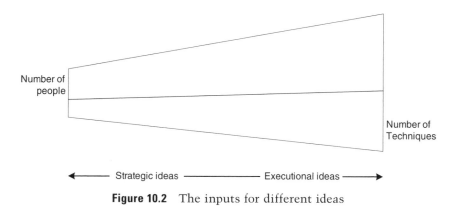

Figure 10.2 The inputs for different ideas

So when developing strategic ideas we believe you need a different mix: a different mix of people and different ways of working.

What follows is our experience of what works. Informed by looking at what ideas are working in the world, and experience on many different brands in many different countries and with many different people. Where we've split techniques between strategic and executional it's for emphasis not exclusion and we're certainly not arrogant enough to suggest these are definitive. However, we are very stubborn on the issue of the number of people. For strategic development, keep it small.

Developing strategic ideas

Building the right team

The best way to develop strategic ideas isn't to appoint an agency but to put together a team. Take the best people out of their agency structures and get them working together. It really works. You don't want a large squad, three is optimal, four at a max. Small teams quickly develop a sense of self and generate their own momentum and with the right skill set, can really deliver. The more you break down the normal boundaries, the better the final product is. The first step is to take people out of their formal structures although this only works if you've got people who were solid enough to begin with. It's critical to get the right type of people – not just people with the right skill set but people with the right level of experience, too. They need to be real experts – the people we call the 'unconsciously competent'.

In learning how to do anything from painting a picture to playing tennis to generating a communication idea, people go through four distinct phases:

Unconscious incompetence – 'I don't know that I don't know what I'm doing'.

Conscious incompetence – 'I know that I don't know what I'm doing'.

Conscious competence – 'I know I know what I'm doing'.

And finally, unconscious competence – 'I just do it'.

So the people who personify the latter are the people you're after. And this is why techniques are secondary to people. We all know the benefit experience brings in solving problems. We can seemingly short cut to an answer, not because any less thought has been applied but because the information and issues have been processed much more quickly, sometimes at a subconscious level.

Skill sets and inputs

There are four key qualities needed in people to produce a 'hard as nails' strategic idea:

1. Insight

2. Through-the-line Activation Experience

3. Creativity

4. Brand Understanding

These qualities are not listed in order of importance, but ranked according to their rarity. In other words, in our opinion, people with genuine insight are the rarest breed, while those with brand understanding are easier to find. We should also be clear that we don't mean that you're looking for four individuals each with a different quality, but rather that you need to be sure that you have these four bases covered somewhere within the team.

Insight

Real insights that can drive strategic ideas are tough to get and often things that are dressed up as insights are little more than common knowledge or simple underdeveloped observations. In his book *Beyond Disruption* Jean-Marie Dru has a great term for these bits of information. He calls them 'Duh!' insights: 'Things that offer no deeper meaning than common knowledge and generic statements about "what people are like" or category-sales attributes'. But some individuals are spectacularly gifted in distilling real insights and this skill is invaluable in creating strategic ideas that are designed to change attitude and behaviour.

Through-the-line activation experience

It's rare to find people who have a breadth and depth of experience in activating brands through-the-line . . . either at a strategic communications planning level, or at a pure executional level. But these people can help enormously because they have an intuitive understanding of how self-expanding an idea is through-the-line.

Creativity

It's a fact that some people are just more creative than others and, on the whole, the more diverse a person's experiences have been, the more creative he or she will tend to be. It's no surprise to us that people who are naturally creative often have unconventional backgrounds or interests. We really think that creative people are made, that they're wired differently because they've done different things.

In other words, the more experiences you have had, the more potential you have. To return to James Webb Young (see Chapter 1) he describes the value of general information in creating ideas by having what he called a 'kaleidoscopic approach' to life.

But let's be absolutely clear here. We're not just talking about advertising agency creatives; all sorts of people can fit the bill as a 'creative'. Often the best account planners fit this description or people from activation or other BTL agencies.

Brand understanding

Whose role is this? One of two people fit this best: an agency account planner or the client. We're very keen that clients are part of the team. All too often great thinking gathers dust in the bottom of a desk drawer, because the decision maker doesn't have a sense of ownership over it – and the simplest way round this is for the client to be co-author. When you've co-created you're much more likely to get momentum and you'll be much better at selling it (which will inevitably be needed internally, if nowhere else). The only problem is that sometimes clients can be obstacles to getting really energetic ideas. It's a cliché, but the type of people who work in client organisations tend to be more corporate than people in agencies. They're more comfortable with process and structure and can often settle for pedestrian ideas because they're comfortable with them, when what's required is an idea that's inherently uncomfortable and challenging.

So, get the elements together and get dedicated to the task. Getting out of the agency environment is really important. Off-site is best but often working in the client office can be really productive. It seems to bring out particular qualities in agency people that are useful in the process. This is partly because it helps them to get really immersed in the task, but partly because agency people like to think of themselves as rather exotic creatures and being in the client's office can make them feel special. But if you can be based off-site so much the better. Holing up somewhere can get the team a real sense of purpose particularly once they've been through the first technique.

So what might the team look like?

A good example of a team of people who would encompass this skill base would be:

- the Creative Director (creativity plus insight);

- the Communications Planner (through-the-line activation experience plus creativity);

- the Marketing Manager (brand understanding);

- the Account Planner (insight plus brand understanding plus creativity).

Four techniques that work well in generating strategic ideas

In this we'll be looking at the purpose (what are they good for) and the method (what do you do). We're clear that techniques are secondary to the people but even when working with the wisest sage it's good to have some way of stimulating and collating the thinking. So let's introduce the four techniques.

1. Immersion

2. Observation insight

3. Brand atomisation

4. ABC^2 (Audience, Brand, Category, Culture)

There's no obligation to practise all four although we'd always encourage you to do the first: it isn't revolutionary, difficult or complicated but it is essential.

Technique 1: Immersion

Objective

To get a real world perspective on your brand, consumers and customers by immersing yourself in the consumer, trade and category. This should generate some tentative thoughts about what your idea could be and help the team to bond.

Method

First and foremost, talk to your consumers and customers. What you are looking for is an understanding of what motivates them in the broadest sense within your category. In addition, you are sure to get great stimulus for other consumer points of influence that weren't apparent before. Talk to consumers and find out your brand's place in their lives. Ask them about emerging trends and concerns, as this will allow your activation to be even more relevant and engaging. What is the most important thing in their lives? What do they do to relax? Where do they seek information? What associations do they have with key brands and icons? When purchasing your brand what would they consider most important – image or value for money? What is different about x brand? What might make them change to another brand in this category? What and who inspires them? What would they buy if they couldn't buy product x? On what occasions do they consume brand y? When talking to the trade you're looking to get an insider's point of view on who is and who isn't buying your product and some understanding of the barriers facing consumption. Look at the communication activity across all brands to get an idea of who's standing out, who's got what type of idea and what you should do to compete. Look for which brands are present, look at merchandising strategy for different retailers, look for promotional ideas, look for areas of display or sale, be that at-shelf, free-standing units or at counter stands by the retail fixture, and observe how shoppers go about choosing product. How much time is spent at fixture? How many items are purchased? How many items are picked up and rejected? How many people read contents and instructions?

Technique 2: Observation insight

Objective

To achieve a gradual distillation from observation to insight to tentative ideas.

Method

This is a process of creating, grouping and distilling. Extract three or four themes that are relevant to the objectives of the brand essence or problem and list two pages of observations per theme, using one team member to facilitate and another to write them up on a flip-chart. In looking for observations, there will be some insights which come out and there should be a couple of people in the team (not the facilitator) to capture them. Once there are 15–20 insights, group them and try to develop a strategic idea for each group.

This is harder than it seems. What's difficult is the early stage: to remove judgements and just stick to pure observations. It's like Gestalt therapy. You don't have an opinion, you don't judge; you just say what you see.

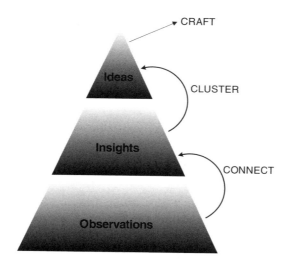

Figure 10.3   Observation insight technique

Technique 3: Brand atomisation

Objective

To see what latent potential lies under the skin of the brand by forensically peeling away its different attributes.

Method

Break the brand down into components (atoms) and for each component, create a funnel that works from the broad brand component towards brand ideas. For example, in our work for Beiersdorf and their brand Nivea Visage, we identified four key components:

Brand atomisation

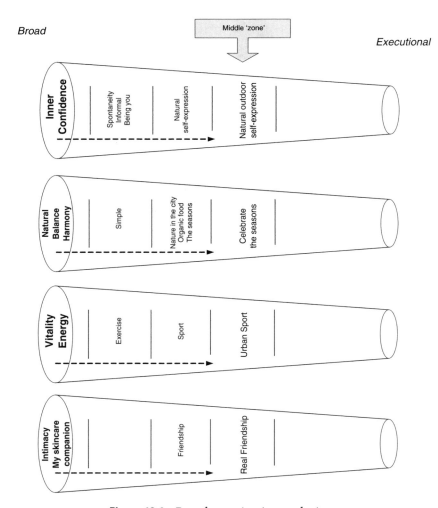

Figure 10.4 Brand atomisation technique

- Intimacy, my skincare companion;

- Natural, down to earth, balance and harmony;

- Vitality and energy;

- Inner confidence.

We then developed funnels for each, with possible strategic ideas identified in the middle zone. This is shown in Figure 10.4 below:

Technique 4: ABC²

Objective

Create ideas that have real world stickiness by examining the Audience, Brand, Category and Culture.

Method

In a rectangle you separately collect all the insight and information you know about:

—Audience: aspirations, motivations, lifestyle, media lives, marital status, occupations, etc.

—Brand: history, product benefits, essence, differentiators, iconography, etc.

—Category: issues, communication norms, ways people buy in the category.

—Culture: established and emergent cultural trends.

Firstly you need to examine these aspects individually; then the fun bit: you collide them together and look for links that might generate strong ideas.

Note: this is covered in more depth in Chapter 11.

Developing executional ideas

As well as coming up with them on your own, implementation ideas are well suited to workshop environments and later in this section we'll talk about a different approach to workshops developed by our sister company, the excellent brand consultancy Added Value. To begin though, we wanted to share with you 10 of the techniques that we use. Some are hard with a concrete output, some softer and some more about pure creative models and attitudes that can help to answer any problem.

There's lots to take in here, but don't worry unduly; because near the end of this chapter (page 217) we've included a summary diagram, that shows which technique will yield which types of ideas.

Ten techniques that work well in developing executional ideas

Creative games

Sitting and staring at a task is a sure-fire way not to achieve it. So let's look at some ways of bringing fresh perspectives and introducing new variables into the creative process, particularly when you are coming up with activation ideas and symbiotic ideas. They all involve three basic steps:

1. Move away from the task and go into a different space   Step back

2. Create new material in the new space   Create

3. Connect the new material back to the task   Collide

There are lots of great creative games to play and a host of books dealing with idea creation, but here are several of our favourite types.

Dimensions

This is a deceptively simple and powerful way of creating ideas, just by looking at things through a different dimension. Ask yourself questions like these:

- What if the brand was 500 years old? What if it was born yesterday?

- What if we only had one person in our target audience?

- What if the idea had to last for a thousand years? What if it lasted for just a moment?

And our favourite:

- What if the budget was £100,000,000? And, of course, what if we had a budget of just £1?

Randomness

This is a game that can feel awkward at first but is very good at creating divergent thinking. First, pick something at random, such as a famous person (living or dead), a fictional character, a colour, a number, a random word from the dictionary or something else random! Then write down all the associations and attributions you have about your random selection. Then relate these back to the task.

This might sound strange but it works. A great example of this technique in action was the development of a contextual framework for an upscale fragrance, created using an unlikely ally – Darth Vader! Here's how the sequence of events went from Darth to idea:

—Darth Vader > Black

—Black > Dark

—Dark > Night

Finally, this was expressed as a contextual framework for the brand: 'The magic of the night'. Would we have got to this point by any other means? It's unlikely. Is it a clear idea? Absolutely. Did we think at the start that Darth Vader had any connection with women's fragrance? Not in the slightest!

Reverse and project

The aim of this kind of game is to make yourself believe that even a bad idea can lead to a good idea and that you can create great ideas just by believing that you can. Here are three examples:

Bad idea – Good idea

Take a piece of paper and, in response to a task, write down the worst ideas you can think of – the real stinkers! Then imagine that your CEO has heard about these ideas and thinks they're brilliant, so that you now have to turn these obviously awful ideas into great ones. As well as being a lot of fun, this is perfect for removing the fear of failure, by turning fear to your advantage.

Heaven – Hell

This is a variation on the game above. Describe the very worst ideas, circumstances and events that lead to brand hell. The next step is to think of new ideas that can help you to avoid this happening. Brand heaven is similar but reversed. Describe brand heaven – what it's like when everything you do is fantastic and goes perfectly (this is often far more challenging to imagine than brand hell!). Then describe the ideas that got you there.

Brand obituary – Celebration speech

In a brand obituary, imagine the brand has died and, going into extreme detail, describe the events that led to its death. Then come up with ideas to make sure it avoids that fate. Alternatively, imagine it's the marketing awards of the year and that your brand has been voted brand of the year for the best consumer engagement. Write a speech describing what activities the brand did to earn such an accolade.

Dressing up

This is a classic example of a 'what if?' game. In this type of exercise, you put on somebody else's clothes and try to see things from their perspective. Here are two variations on the theme.

Corporate takeover

Imagine that your brand has been taken over by another organisation. Describe the philosophy and the attributes that you associate with the new organisation and come up with ways of activating your brand in the light of these. The best type of companies to use are those that are well defined, imaginative, varied and successful. Classics for this task are: Apple, Coca-Cola, Nike, Virgin, Orange, Chanel and PlayStation.

Class act

In this variation use an individual rather than a company – someone such as your favourite actor, director or artist who is renowned for their creativity. Again describe their attributes and think about what ideas they would have for the brand.

Connection point exploration

Purpose

To identify physical and emotional contexts that influence the consumer in your category.

Application

This technique is great for finding contextual frameworks and symbiotic ideas.

Method

Finding connection points is an exploration of when the consumer is most open to the brand message. These points are very specific – a certain situation rather than a broad channel and although they often cannot be bought, this exercise is good for warming up and getting into the right frame of mind.

So, look for connection points under these headers:

- Circumstances;

- Environments and places;

- Frames of mind;

- Times of day/days of week;

- Seasons;

- Occasions.

Then make a list of circumstances and places, using a form like this:

Circumstances	
Places	
Frames of mind	
Environments	

Figure 10.5 Connection Points based on circumstances and places

And finally think about contact timing: are there ideal times for your message to be received?

Brand behaviour rules

Purpose

To ensure that the brand articulates itself cohesively in the marketplace.

Application

This technique is very good for developing contextual frameworks and symbiotic ideas. It is also very useful in guiding strategy and as an inspiration for activation ideas. Having a distinctive behavioural checklist is also a healthy test of

Times of day / days of week	
Seasons	
Occasions	

Figure 10.6 Connection Points based on timing

current activity. Is it right? Does it still fit the new desires for the brand? Is it time to let go?

Method

Rules should be tight enough to define the right brand behaviour and broad enough to have longevity, for example for Pilsner Urquell (beer), one of the behaviour rules is 'adopt the behaviour of premium whisky'. You should use the strategic idea and brand essence as a stimulus to define what communication behaviour the brand should or shouldn't do. From this long list, you should then select four to six rules that do not overlap and give a strong tonal sense of what the communication activity should be like.

Output

A set of four to six clear behavioural rules that create a distinctive voice in the market place and stimulate great executional ideas.

Target market trends

Purpose

To understand what the emerging behaviours and attitudes are for your audience in order to ensure your communication activity has maximum relevance.

Application

Identifying established trends has an obvious application in creating activation ideas. But it's more interesting to try to lock down emergent trends, and getting the brand involved in the early expressions of the cultural movements is a powerful way to create activation ideas that give the brand energy and relevance.

Grabbing these sorts of trends can say more about the brand than any other form of activity. They bring the brand into the here and now in a way that's meaningful and engaging. Activation through emergent trends truly helps the brand to find its voice with consumers.

Method

An obvious place to start is to review any trend documents relating to your target audience that are available. Advertising agencies, brand consultants, research companies and media owners are ideal sources. The web is also a fantastic tool for studying consumer trends, so read the blogs and messaging boards of the different groups you're targeting and check sites such as MySpace. Of course, the real advantage of the web is that as well as reading you can also post your own questions. Lastly, meet with the editors of media that the target market consume as they will have a great understanding of their consumers and any trends in that market.

Output

Quantitative and qualitative understanding of target market trends and some smart activation ideas.

Take a 3D view of the target audience

Purpose

To create a summary description of your target audience that shows a deep and richer understanding beyond demographics that the team can understand and refer to.

Application

Developing activation ideas.

Method

Nothing beats getting out and talking to consumers, but capturing that information in a distinctive way can consolidate learning and stimulate great ideas. Here are a couple of ways to do this.

A pen portrait

Write a one page summary of a consumer. Give them a name and define their demographics. Write down their lifestyle, attitudes, motivations and needs, as well as the products they consume in specific need states. You should also include potential relevant consumer points of influence.

A day in the life video

Produce a short video on a day in the life of the consumer described in the pen portrait. Follow them through their typical day (this is really useful if you want to brief other members of the company, such as sales people or other agencies).

Another variation on this technique is to mind map the degrees of influence.

Kaleidoscopic mind

Purpose

To be able to have more ideas – faster.

Application

All types of ideas.

Method

This isn't really a technique – more of an approach to life. We've already mentioned a number of times that some people are more 'creative' than others and if there's common ground between these types of people, it's that they have a variety of sometimes eccentric interests – and a real fascination in the world around them.

To return to James Webb Young (see Chapter 1) for the last time, a new idea is the result of a new combination. So the more variables, the more inputs you have, the more possible combinations you can create. The problem is that we all lead busy lives and it's easy to stay in your comfort zone, which is not necessarily conducive to having great ideas. So why not try doing something a little bit different? For example:

- Read a different newspaper.

- Read the bit of the newspaper you normally ignore.

- Listen to a different radio station.

- Buy an album by a band you've never heard of.

- Visit the second city in a country you've never been to.

- Walk a different way to work.

- Go a different route on your lunchtime stroll (in fact we found the BBC Four bench symbiotic idea by doing just that).

Alternatively, with a little more investment of time, one excellent way of broadening your mind is to adopt a genius. Read all you can about the great minds and their work.

Lastly there are some great books in this area. A couple we'd consider 'must reads' are: Jack Foster's *How To Get Ideas*, and Alan Fletcher's *The Art of Looking Sideways*. The latter is an absolute visual feast of a book, totally unique and brimming with terrific stimulus; but a word of warning, because it's very addictive and is a bigger stealer of time than 'Grand Theft Auto'.

Output

A knowledgeable open mind that's sharp at creating ideas.

Steal, steal and steal some more

Purpose

Use the good stuff that's already out there and make it your own.

Application

All executional ideas, in particular activation ideas

Method

This is a way of collecting all of the great executional ideas that you see around you.

And there is nothing wrong with stealing, as long as you make it your own. As Voltaire once said:

Originality is nothing more than judicious imitation.

There are some great examples of ideas that have transferred across categories and have even inspired entire companies. In John Grant's *The Brand Innovation Manifesto*, he describes how Innocent Drinks is really a copy of Ben and Jerry's transferred to smoothies. There are also some magazines that are brilliant for this exercise, in particular Benetton's 'Colors', 'Cream', and 'Contagious', all of which are 'idea candy'.

One tip is to buy a spare hard drive and dedicate it to your collection. We both own a treasure chest of brilliant ideas in our remote hard drives in a box the size of a pack of cards and at a cost of under £80.

Output

A great library of inspiration that you can use to create your own ideas.

Double bubbles

Purpose

To create ideas rooted in the brand and the consumer.

Application

Creating activation ideas.

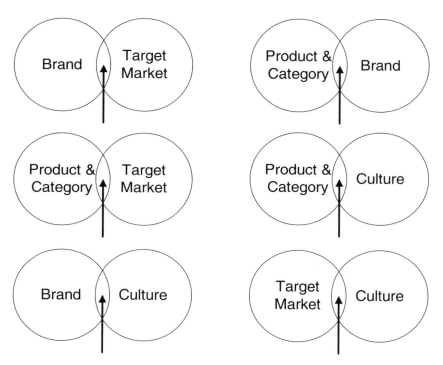

Figure 10.7 Double Bubbles

Method

This is another technique that can be used as an individual or in groups. It's a simplification of the ABC^2 technique for creating strategic ideas and in this case you juxtapose information in two overlapping bubbles and look for the connectors. Of course, anything can be compared within the two bubbles but normally brand and target market work best for developing activation ideas, although you can also combine brand and category as well as category and target market when you're delving for insights.

When you're using the brand and target audience for activation ideas the key ingredient is the strategic idea so, as you can imagine, this is best when dealing with brand ideas and emotional platforms rather than physical platforms which are three-quarters there already. Within the audience bubble you should look at aspirations, motivations, pastimes, lifestyle, influencers and everything else you've found out along the way.

Output

Activation ideas that have relevance and – who knows? – perhaps an original insight!

Purchase pathway

Purpose

Create tight ideas by using the different stages of consumer purchase.

Application

Useful for symbiotic ideas, contextual frameworks and for identifying points at which you might activate. It's also good for mapping out your completed strategy, plan and activity so you can see where you expect it to have an effect.

Method

Use your understanding of the target audience and category to isolate the separate steps to purchase – the purchase pathway

– from early consideration right up to the moment of purchase. Based on an understanding of each stage in the purchase pathway, you can identify potential connection points for contextual frameworks, symbiotic ideas and activation ideas. It could be that you already have extensive research for the separate steps for your market but if not, use your common sense and the qualitative and quantitative work you've completed to make them up. Here are some example steps:

- Awareness – consideration – trial – usage – loyalty;

- Sample – attitude – re-sample – purchase – loyalty;

- Attention – consideration – purchase – loyalty;

- Loyalty – drop out – re-experience – loyalty.

The real value of this technique is not in the broader steps themselves but in the detail within each step – the separate connections points.

Output

Ideas that drive behavioural change and are a smart way of analysing and presenting your plan.

Mind mapping

Purpose

To explore how a core idea can be expanded.

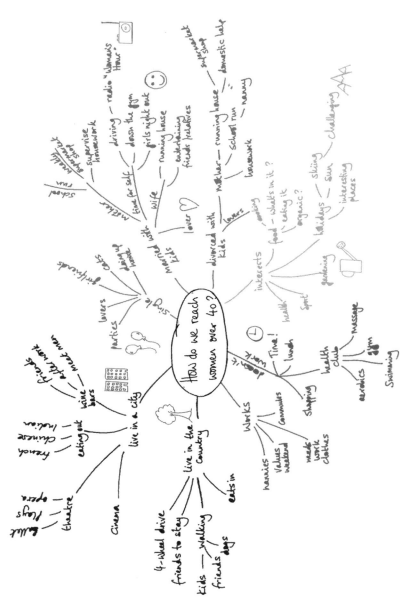

Figure 10.8 Mind mapping

Application

This is a well-established technique, applicable to any idea, not just for communications, although it is particularly useful for developing contextual frameworks and activation ideas.

Method

Mind-mapping entails putting a key word or thing in the middle of a piece of paper – normally on a flip-chart – and then spinning off ideas associated with it. The sort of words or things that can be interrogated in this way include:

- Brand essence, discriminator or functional benefit, key brand benefit;

- Brand idea; or advertising idea;

- Target: How do you reach them? Their attitudes to channels, their passion points.

Output

Ideas that are beyond the obvious, worked up in some detail.

Finally . . . we can now summarise the different techniques and how they best relate to idea types.

	Emotional Platforms	Brand Ideas	Physical Platforms	Advertising Ideas	Activation Ideas	Symbiotic Ideas	Contextual Frameworks
Immersion	○	○	○	○	○	○	○
Category Observation	○	○	○	○			
Funnel	○	○	○		○		
ABC²	○	○		○			
Creative Games				○	○	○	
Connection Point			○		○	○	○
Brand Behavioural Rules				○		○	○
Target Market Trends					○		
3D View				○	○		○
Kaleidoscopic Mind	○	○	○	○	○	○	
Stealing			○	○	○	○	
Double Bubble					○	○	
Purchase Pathway					○	○	○
Mind Mapping			○	○	○		○

Figure 10.9 Summary of techniques

Workshops

Making workshops work

We're not fans of the term 'brainstorm' not because of the PC concerns but because it's a cliché, it's uninspiring and it's actually wrong. Brainstorms are like a bunch of penniless kids poring over a Chinese menu: they come up with a long list of things that they'd like, but they know all along that nothing is ever going to happen. They might enjoy it at the time, but they still end up hungry. The missing dimension in many executional workshops is the same that's missing in strategic ideas – a process of refinement. So we use Added Value's *Generator* technique that brings in time for critical judgement.

Basic workshop smarts:

There are many ways to run a workshop and what follows are hints and tips on how to make yours as successful as it can be.

- Invite a diverse group of people all of whom must have the desire to produce great ideas.

- Hold the workshop in a great venue off-site, to break people out of their comfort zone, never use the office boardroom. The venue should be light, airy and not corporate.

- If you can, make sure the venue is relevant to the brand or consumer.

- Have a fabulous facilitator – either someone from the core team or separate from the core team.

- During the workshop, get people to work individually and in groups and be sure to mix up the groups.

Workshop participation:

There are four golden rules to establish for participation in a workshop:

1. Active listening – participants should be encouraged to actively listen in the workshop when others are speaking and not become too focused on their own work.

2. The tools of the workshop are felt-tip pens and Post-it notes. Which leads into rule three . . .

3. When writing an idea on a Post-it note, participants should be encouraged to write a headline that captures the essence of the thought and to only have one thought per Post-it note (fat pens and small spaces mean you're more likely to write the essentials).

4. When ideas are being presented back to the group, and participants have a strong positive, or negative reaction to the idea, they should be encouraged to do a 'how to' or a 'build'. So, if a participant loves an idea and feels that they could contribute to make it richer, they can write their suggestion on a Post-it note and stick it on top of the original idea. A 'how to' is useful if a participant has a negative reaction to an idea. The group should also be

encouraged to think about how they could turn an idea that they disagree with into a positive, actionable idea.

Structuring the workshop:

The best way to structure a workshop across a day is as a diamond pattern – begin with a brief introduction, introduce the exercises to encourage creative thinking and then filter the ideas to end up with three or four excellent, actionable ideas. This is the really critical phase as it's where the judgement of the group is brought to bear.

The workshop flow:

A warm-up helps get people into the right frame of mind, so do something creative. For example, get people to draw some-

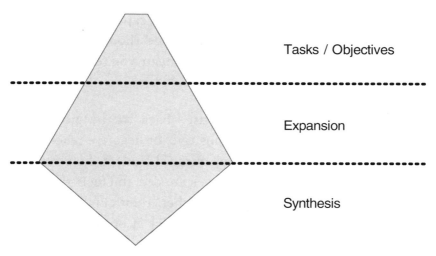

Tasks / Objectives

Expansion

Synthesis

Figure 10.10 Structuring a workshop

thing. This can be something that relates to the task of the workshop or something from their day to day lives (e.g. draw the best piece of advice you were ever given). Then get them to present their pictures back to the group.

The next step is for the brand manager or communication planner to give a short introduction to the task.

A useful next step is to do the 'brainbank' – asking people to write down their gut responses to the task and to present each thought back to the group.

Next divide people into groups and get them thinking. This is where you can use the creative games described earlier in this chapter, but don't forget that yes you want to create divergence but the real value comes from relating that thinking back to the tasks.

The final phase of the workshop is filtering all the ideas that have been generated. Here there are two techniques that can be used:

The first is to split the group into two teams. Then get each team to decide what they feel are the three most powerful ideas and get them to present a formal argument on why those should be the ideas that get taken forward. The other team should listen to the argument and argue against them. The best ideas should win the day.

The other technique is to get each person to mark the three ideas that they feel are the most powerful. The three or four ideas with most votes are the ones that get taken forward. In addition to the ideas that are being taken forward, it is a good idea to type up and share all of the material produced as it may be useful later on.

Lastly, if you can, video people presenting the ideas during the session as this makes great presentation collateral.

A final word

Of all the techniques and stimulus at our disposal it's worth saying how important the role of alcohol can be. This isn't a joke. Alcohol is the unsung hero of creativity. Not getting

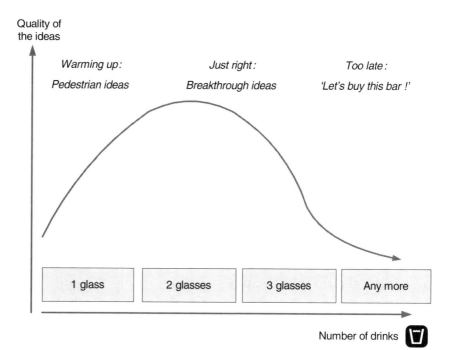

Figure 10.11 The Magic Second Drink

hammered (although we did think about creating a technique that included drinking three shots of whisky every ten minutes and drawing your idea after each one) but being in that middle zone.

When teams have spent the whole day stoking themselves full of insight, brand experience and tentative ideas, it's often in the bar after the second glass when the sparks start to fly and the breakthroughs occur. And we said that the more you can deconstruct, the more barriers you remove, the better the output and that hour over a glass or two can be the time when real magic is made. Just don't forget your pen!

11

Judging brand ideas: trout or trolley?

JUDGING BRAND IDEAS IS A BIT LIKE FISHING IN A CITY stream. You cast your line into the murky water and you feel a sudden tug. You pull on it and your pulse starts racing – because it feels like something big. You brace yourself and slowly, slowly reel it in, becoming ever more convinced that this time you really have caught a whopper. But it won't be until you finally get it to the surface that you'll know whether all that patience and all that struggle have paid off. Have you caught the prize trout you always dreamt of, or is it just another shopping trolley?

Our urban fisherman can always toss the trolley back (or return it to Tesco round the corner), but with a brand idea it's not quite as simple as that. Because with a brand idea the real moment of truth only comes when the idea goes to market, by which time, of course, it's far too late to toss it back. Too much time and money will already have been spent; too much will be tied up with it. So when you're developing a brand idea, you really need to know what's on the end your line before you get it to the surface. Is this the kind of magical brand idea that will guarantee solid gold top line growth for your brand? Or is it just a flimsy emotional platform? Or an advertising idea masquerading as something else? In short, whenever you think you've hooked a brand idea, you need to know – is this a trout or a trolley?

But peering into that murky water and trying to work out exactly what you've caught is no easy matter. So in this chapter, we're going to examine the issues involved in judging brand ideas and offer some practical advice, along with some examples of how it can be done.

Understanding the elements

Let's assume, based on the Higher Order Communication Objective thinking outlined in Chapter 9, that you have decided that you need a brand idea.

When you then try to develop it, and are looking around for inspiration, you need to pick up on the ABC^2 technique touched on in the previous chapter.

You need to begin with three basic elements that should go into a brand idea – the ABC – and these are:

—Audience: what are some genuine insights or consumer truths about this consumer?

—Brand: what is it about the brand or its history that is interesting and unique?

—Category: what category is it in and what are its usage occasions?

These three elements should always be part of a brand idea. If they are not, you can run into trouble. Take Benetton, for example. We would guess that their brand idea has been 'Open minds' or 'Tolerance' (and in fact these are so broad that they are probably better described as emotional platforms). But ten years ago, a global advertising idea called 'Shock' was used, which presented images of black and white horses mating, nuns kissing priests and dying HIV victims. It excited a lot of interest at the time, but the problem was, what did it have to do with Benetton's products? Just go and look at them in a shop and there is nothing cutting edge about them: lots of lollipop-coloured, expensive sweaters, often worn by European businessmen at the weekend! The communications set the consumer up for a serious disappointment.

So the lesson is, never stray outside the orbit of the category, the product and its usage occasions. This doesn't mean that you always have to show a product being used; it simply means that you shouldn't expect consumers to make a huge leap. They need to be able to understand the linkage between the idea and the product. If your product is beer, for example, a brand idea about 'talking' would be fine. It might not link directly to the product, but consumers understand the connection between talking and beer.

Audience, brand and category are all crucial elements. But there is also a fourth element, which is equally important – and this fourth element completes our ABC^2:

—Culture: is there a cultural trend that is emerging?

Why has Dove's 'Real Beauty' worked so well? It is because the brand idea is based on a cluster of increasingly relevant cultural insights – that people want more realism, that they are increasingly immune to all the fads and fakes in the world and that women in particular, are tired of the fashion magazine image of themselves and want a more honest definition of beauty.

Another example is Visa Europe and its brand idea, called 'Love Every Day'. This idea is all about inspiring people to enjoy the simple pleasures of life. So it's about celebrating the everyday things – like the glass of wine after a hard day's work – that are actually more important than the bigger things – like going on holiday – and so make a real difference. And this resonates well in today's world because it is these everyday pleasures which are either taken for granted nowadays, or which fall by the wayside in our busy lives.

Apple's brand idea also works well – the notion that 'Man Is Not Subservient To Technology'. The point of view is simple: technology will take over if you let it, and we will be enslaved by it – think of Blackberries and how often people look at them at the weekend. So rather than build technology that undermines us as people, Apple want to build technology that liberates our souls.

Figure 11.1   Visa in Ireland and Love Every Journey

These three brand ideas have a philosophy at their core which resonates with societal and cultural reality of today.

The diagram opposite shows the four basic elements as a 'frame'.

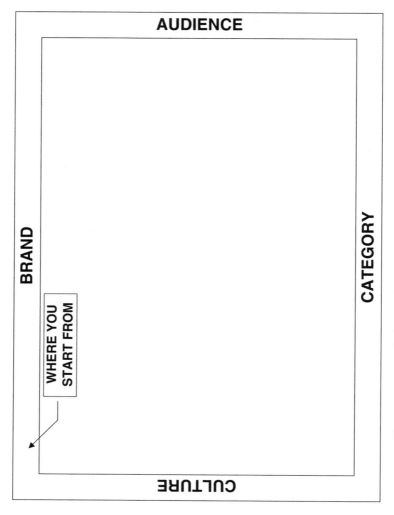

Figure 11.2 Brand Ideas – the raw materials that create the 'frame'

So if these are the elements, how do you judge the potential brand ideas that you come up with by playing with them? When do you know if a potential idea is a 'hit' or a 'miss'? A trout or a trolley? Figure 11.3 overleaf shows this as a target, with cross-hairs.

The seven qualities of trout

If your brand idea really is a prize trout, it will have these seven qualities that you should be able to feel tugging on the line.

Clarity

The idea will be clear. When you write it down as a sentence, it will not be convoluted, nor will it try to bolt two or three things together with no real focus. People who are not directly involved in its creation – like the CEO, for example – should be able to understand it immediately.

Rootedness

It will be fundamentally rooted in the brand and product; it will make sense in terms of where the brand has been historically and the link to the product category will be easy and natural to the consumer.

Legs

Yes, this trout needs legs! By that we mean the idea should be self-expanding and that executional ideas will drip off it

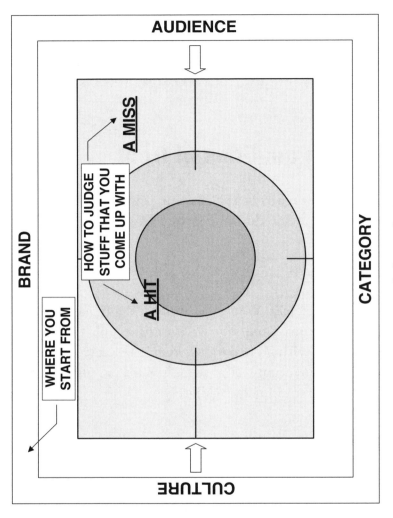

Figure 11.3 Brand Ideas – The Cross-Hairs

like ripe fruit from a tree. Although don't confuse executional ideas, with the executions themselves. It's easy for an agency to show a dozen executions off a proposed brand idea, through-the-line, on TV and outdoor and in-store and at an event. However, this is not a test of a brand idea. This may be simply about taking a single visual device and using it in many different ways. What we are talking about here is different. We are talking about genuine executional ideas – and activation ideas in particular. If the brand idea is really good, you should be able to generate 50 activation ideas off it.

Depth

By depth, we mean that you will be able to work out how to evolve the idea, how to sequence it and layer it, so that it maintains its interest to consumers over the longer term. This can sometimes be an issue. You might have a simple idea that everyone understands, but if it also lacks depth then the executional ideas you come up with will be the same type year after year. The brand idea will not have a natural layering to it, which will mean that to the consumer, the idea will get boring before long.

Energy

A good brand idea will have energy within it and will be inherently interesting. At first sight it might even be a little scary. But it will mean that those charged with execution, in whatever form, will be itching to work on it!

Challenge

It will also reframe the competition. It will say, we refuse to believe that this category is low-interest to consumers. We refuse to accept the communication rules that the others all play by – like simply dramatising the product or product benefit. It will find a territory within the orbit of the product, that others have overlooked.

Definition

Lastly, and most importantly, it will be in the right idea 'zone': it will be in a well-defined, tangible area, that you can get your arms around.

Some practical assessments

Unfortunately, there are far more trolleys out there than trout. We would estimate that three-quarters of the ideas out there, purporting to be brand ideas, are actually not. There are two reasons for this. Firstly it's because coming up with good brand ideas is actually very, very hard. And secondly, very often those judging them aren't really qualified to do so, as they have don't have enough experience of working with ideas through-the-line.

So to help understand the difficulties and the ways a potential brand idea might miss the mark, let's analyse the following sets of words. We will judge these in the abstract – unconnected to any individual brand or category and mark them according to how well they perform as brand ideas.

A new spirit in fragrance

Do you understand this line? What type of spirit are we talking about? There's nothing here that would get us interested. The double-meaning of 'spirit' (i.e. that fragrance is also alcohol) makes this a good pay-off line. But it's not an idea.

Score: 1/10

Make history

This is obviously a call to action, to do something that makes history. It feels like it's asking us to do something. But it doesn't give any sense of what that is. It's not clear what it pertains to. Make history, how? It feels initially interesting, but then, on closer inspection, it lets you down. As it is, it's an attitudinal statement, which makes for a good pay-off line. But without more context, it's not a brand idea. It might also be dangerous in certain categories, especially for relatively superficial products. Imagine seeing 'Toothpaste X "Makes History"'! You'd think it was a bit of a joke at best; at worst it would be really annoying. The dissonance between the truth and the claim would be just too great.

Score: 3/10

Purity

Purity probably makes you think of Evian. But that aside, as a potential idea, we think it's got some scope. There's something nice, there. Purity, nowadays, has some rarity. And you can apply it in almost any area; you can look at things in their purest form.

So it is fine as something a brand can stand for. However, it's still too broad to give real direction to a brand's communication. It's too 'fat'. If you were to ask ten people to activate it, they'd probably go in very different directions. Furthermore, we think it's an area where you might run out of steam quite quickly in executional terms.

Score: 5/10

Inner strength

'Inner Strength' is the sort of brand idea that comes out of just a little too much focus on the consumer and consumer insight. The problems with it are two-fold. Firstly, to connect with someone's inner strength is difficult on a mass level. Inner strength is a personal thing – a moment of inner strength might be when you're about to sit an exam. Or when someone you know has died. Or a spouse has left you. But as a brand, how do you connect with these moments, en masse, and would you want to? Secondly, to bring it to life, you might want to dramatise it using a situation between people that would require the use of film. So it is really an advertising idea. To take inner strength through-the-line would necessitate a better mechanic, like 'Stories of inner strength' which would also get around the first problem – and take it away from being personal.

For us great brand ideas are self-supporting. They don't need other things to keep them aloft. They have their own power source. So in this case, 'Inner strength' is not a particularly good brand idea, because it needs something else to help it.

Score: 4/10

Journeys

This could lead to some pretty good activation ideas and it's an area where content is easy to come by. But it is just too broad to be useful. There are simply too many types of journey, both physical and spiritual. But if it was, for example, 'Personal journeys' or 'Journeys that changed your life' then this would give it the right amount of focus – placing it in the right sort of executional 'zone'. You might also want to give it a category twist, so for a chocolate bar it might become 'Journeys of love'.

Score: 6/10

Intelligent choice

Intelligent choice is not so much broad, as vague. As planners we don't understand what to do with it, because intelligent choices are 'in the eye of the beholder'. And opinions as to what constitutes an intelligent choice will differ from person to person. Also, to bring something like this to life will probably require dramatisation using a situation involving people and narrative, which only film can provide.

There's also not enough tension between the two words; there's no 'flint versus steel' to create the spark. It's a bit bland. But then again, it's something no brand would disagree with! 'Intelligent choice, oh yes, that's us!'

Score: 2/10

Don't compromise

This could be quite good. It has a point of view. It's focused. Very quickly you start thinking about people who don't compromise, and what you respect about them. More often than not, people who don't compromise have done great things in the world. You could play with this easily through-the-line. And for advertising alone it would work well. 'Don't compromise' almost demands situations where alternatives are set up before you, and you demonstrate resolve by not compromising. Where it could fail is in fast moving consumer goods categories and things that are everyday choices. After all, some things are actually worth compromising, because they're not really that important. So this idea needs something with a high price tag.

Score: 7/10

You never forget your first . . .

This is a classic case of an advertising idea, masquerading as a brand idea. It's simply impossible to take through-the-line.

And very much like the example above, this claim might be true for, say, a Jaguar car; but it's not the case if we're talking about your first packet of Smarties!

Score: 3/10

Work to live!

This is a good brand idea, because it is short, it's got energy, it has a point of view and it runs against the conventional current of society, where too many people live to work. So it feels resonant. It's also fairly easy to think of activation ideas. The brand might develop something around a 'Three-day weekend'. Another one might be 'Well leave', where you get days off work when you're feeling fantastic, not sick. Basically, this is a good example of a potential brand idea.

Score: 8/10

Refreshing thoughts

This is the result of trying to build an emotional proposition for a brand, while still remaining rooted in the functional product benefit (which is obviously for a drink). So, how good is it as a brand idea? Can you think of some refreshing thoughts? How many? It's clear that this could make a good brand idea, but it might be demanding to execute, if you rely just on the agency. However, if you could co-opt the consumer in defining 'refreshing thoughts', then coming up with lots of them might not be an issue and they might turn out to be really interesting and fun.

Score: 7/10

Great friendships

This is not a break-out thought but it's a reasonable brand idea. And by defining the type of friendship as 'great friendship' it gains the right level of focus and tangibility, while still allowing scope for interesting execution. You could explore types of great friendships, for example or you could dramatise famous friendships – like between Matt Damon and Ben Affleck. But really, to bring the brand into the here and now, you would want to empower consumers to create great friendships between themselves. The only real issue for this potential brand idea is that 'friendship' is quite a generic area for brands to play in.

Score: 7/10

The most loved French icon

This feels like a statement, as opposed to an idea. It would be tricky to execute, because it doesn't even allow for comparisons with other French icons. And in any case, how many French icons are there? Not more than a couple of years' worth, probably.

Score: 1/10

France's best

This one is a claim which might make for a reasonable pay-off line, if it were true. However, even as a pay-off line it would be uninspiring and uninteresting to consumers and it would need constant 'gold medal' type product ads to support it.

Score: 3/10

Secretly taking over the world

This one would actually make a fantastic brand idea for the right brand. It says: you and your brand are engaged in a secret plot to colonise the world. We quite like the tension between 'taking over the world' and 'secrecy'. You could easily engage consumers with this, by developing a series of plots. It could have several layers and could be funny and inspiring to work on.

But as we mentioned, it would only work for the right brand. It needs a brand that has a sense of humour to it. It also needs a brand that is emergent in whatever category it's in. It's not something that can be applied in all brand situations and would probably need a product with some real advantage. What products or brands can you think of which might work here?

Score: 9/10

Celebrating stubbornness

This one would also make a very good brand idea. Stubbornness is fundamentally interesting and the idea of celebrating it is fun and goes against the mainstream; basically, as an idea it bottles energy. Coming off this potential idea, you can see all sorts of fun activation ideas. You might find and uphold stubborn people or celebrate the most stubborn people in history. You could build an activation idea around 'Why stubbornness is a virtue'. You could campaign for 'Stubborn Sundays'. And so on.

Stubbornness is nice because it's tangible. It's something you can get your hands around. And you can really dramatise it in an interesting way.

Score: 9/10

Planned randomness

This potential idea is like the 'shuffle' button on your iPod. It advocates controlled or purposeful randomness. It's about smashing things together . . . to create new combinations. And this would appeal to younger consumers. For an eighteen year old, at this stage in his or her life, nothing is determined. Furthermore, it links to social navigation or fluidity which is how 18 year olds generally like to operate in the evening. It's all about being eclectic and open; and not letting too much logic dictate what you do, where you go, what you decide.

This could be easy to work with. It's very interactive. For example, you might give people a newspaper and let them rearrange it. You might let people randomise words, music collections, stories; in fact, any content, to create something new. We would provide the tools.

Score: 8/10

Figure 11.4 below shows the criteria that make a potential idea a 'hit' or a 'miss'.

And, for the potential ideas we've just looked at, Figure 11.5 shows how they could be placed on this grid.

Developing a new brand idea

Now let's look again at some potential brand ideas, but this time, centred on one brand or product category. In this case – to avoid infringing any client's confidentiality – we'll use a hypothetical one. We're going to look at developing a brand idea for a hypothetical male face care brand. This could be a shaving brand or a skincare brand, it doesn't really matter. And let's say this brand, in personality terms to consumers, is accessible, reliable, masculine, and caring.

We will look at eight potential brand ideas. And for each, we will give a 'stream of thoughts', to illustrate the difficulties you can come up against.

The language of face care

What is the thinking behind this idea? Well, many categories evolve because of a new language (and therefore interest) that is created around the category – coffee and wine are both good examples. Coffee back in 1980 was, well, just coffee, wasn't it? And look at it now – lattes, macchiato, and baristas. So at the heart of this idea is a need to grow the category, and the brand within it, by creating a new language around face care, and in so doing, making it more interesting to men.

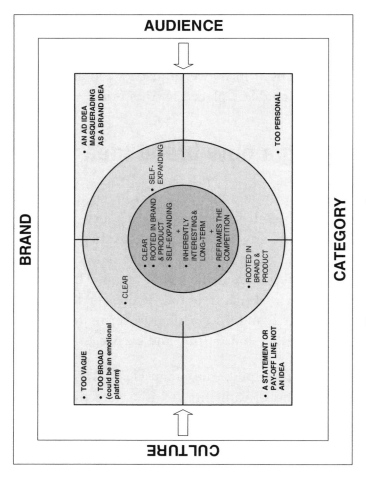

Figure 11.4 Hitting and missing

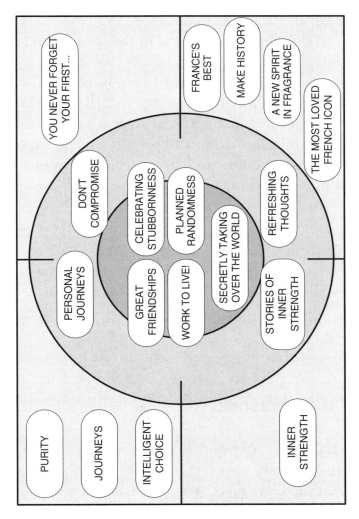

Figure 11.5 Placing our hypothetical Brand Ideas

In terms of execution, you would have to do this in a fun way. You could get the public involved in the creation and naming of products and ways to use products. You could create new occasion-related special packs. It would be possible to do this in an interesting and fun way through-the-line. There are many positives for this idea. It is an original and fresh way of building interest in the category. It's quite focused and could engage the target and create word of mouth. And by suggesting 'new occasions', it could help drive frequency of product use.

And what might be some negatives? Well, there are no real negatives to this idea, other than the fact that many clients would consider it 'too big' an idea for themselves.

Score: 8/10

Mental gymnastics

This idea is less strategic, and is not rooted in any great category-related ambition. It is simply 'about men'. It recognises that men love facts, lists, top tens and mental puzzles. They are all 'guy things'.

This would be a very easy idea to execute. It could be done by giving guys the (branded) tools, via puzzles in print or computer games, IQ testing, and logic games, that might be delivered at home via the internet, or at point of sale. Or it could be done using interactive six-sheet outdoor posters, that are touch-screen, or mobile phone-enabled or through top and tail ads on TV.

So, it's easy to work with and it's directional. But what becomes apparent quickly is how two-dimensional and boring the idea actually is. It's not emotional enough. And to make matters worse, it commits the most cardinal of sins. It's forgotten the product and the usage occasion. It's not rooted in these basics.

Score: 3/10

Facial fashion

The thinking here might be as follows: most men don't naturally think about appearance in terms of 'face' or they see it as something that is 'neutral', and not something that they particularly have to look after, unlike their bodies or their hair. Furthermore, men actually enjoy experimenting and playing with facial hair. It links to vanity, a need for 'camouflage', and wanting change in life. Men are curious to know what they'd look like – they see someone in the street or in a movie, with a certain style of facial hair, and they wonder how they'd look with the same style. In fact, guys have relatively few things about their appearance they can play with. They don't have the same avenues as women. But a lot of guys are quite reserved about 'playing with their faces', particularly in terms of growing a beard of some sort. They worry that it won't look cool, or about the 'growing' period when it'll look a bit of a mess. Hence the 'holiday' phenomena – over a holiday period, how many men have grown a goatee, sideburns or a beard of some sort, only to shave it off the morning they go back to work?

So executing this idea might involve getting guys to enjoy their faces – visually – via creating and leveraging different 'facial fashions'. We could discuss naming existing facial fashions or create facial fashion shows. What about leveraging it on radio, by getting DJs to grow their beards and have fun? Or the equivalent on TV with TV presenters? We could create an annual competition to come up with a new style. Or find and sponsor a character like Ben Stiller in 'Zoolander'!

It works in many respects. It is focused, original and fresh. It would probably engage the target and get some word of mouth going. And it would be easy to activate. But there are a couple of drawbacks. Firstly, it comes at the category issues a bit too laterally – it doesn't really help promote shaving or face products. It also lacks depth, and is quite young in appeal.

Score: 7/10

Setting life goals

Most men don't really think ahead both in life and when it comes to their faces. They are not worried about getting older in terms of looks, and are reactive rather than proactive concerning face care products. They buy the products when they have a problem, and if they don't, they don't think they need them.

So the thought here would be to try to get men to think and plan ahead. But rather than tackle it in terms of 'planning ahead' – which is an uninteresting proposition – we should think about 'setting life goals', which is bigger and a bit more engaging. And indeed, the interesting thing is that the act of defining life goals, actually makes you much more likely to achieve them.

In terms of execution, in print we might create male treasure maps with male future dreams displayed. Online, we could create a 'setting life goals' consulting site. We might also set up a free telephone service, which would help individuals to set goals.

This idea links strongly to the 'care' attribute of the brand, as well as addressing a category barrier. But fundamentally, it is a bit worthy and boring. It would also be hard to do well and could be expensive.

Score: 4/10

Male books

What of this one? Well, it's clearly a physical platform, not a brand idea. As a territory for a brand, it's original. It would be interesting to see a face care brand with a branded display stand in a book-store. That said, it's not dynamic and it really doesn't link well to the product.

Score: N/A (on inspection it turns out not to be a brand idea)

Cycling

This one is also a physical platform. In this case, it's more modern than male books and connects better to the category. It's also a sport 'on the up', both in terms of spectators and participants. To bring alive the territory of cycling, the brand could create annual 'named' events around capital cities; it could sponsor a racing team. Or it might bring alive activation ideas such as 'Take your bike to work'.

Score: N/A (on inspection it turns out not to be a brand idea)

Modern day Dad

This is probably more of an emotional platform than a brand idea, as it's very broad. But it might have merit for a face care brand, because it could represent a 'contemporary male life-style'. Bringing alive this emotional platform could be a little challenging, because there are many interpretations as to what it means to be a modern day Dad. But presumably, taking the kids to school, changing nappies and things like that would be on the cards!

Score: N/A (on inspection it turns out not to be a brand idea)

1,000 faces

This is an ad idea. The thought behind it could be that showing lots of ordinary faces, each one saying 'I use (. . . brand)' will help create the perception amongst guys that the product is becoming widely used, which might help drive product penetration and trial.

It could be executed with a massive back-lit six-sheet outdoor campaign or as an A5 booklet that becomes a print insert. Also, how about some downloadable wallpaper, showing lots of faces?

Score: N/A (on inspection it turns out not to be a brand idea)

A new way of working

As an author of a potential brand idea, you can assess the idea as we've discussed, thinking about what the idea really is, and how empowering it is. And, indeed, as a judge of a potential brand idea, you can do the same. However, in a common client (marketer) and agency scenario, it's not quite so simple.

Usually, the client will brief the agency (it could be one of several types), who will go away and consider maybe half a dozen ideas all of which may have great potential. It will then settle on one, perhaps because it has found a great way to execute it. Then the agency will return to the client and sell its potential brand idea with gusto. It'll create a sense of theatre around the insight or reason the idea will connect deeply with the target consumer. And then it'll show lots of executions that derive from the brand idea, starting maybe with a TV ad, and moving on to other elements, showing the visual synergy across them.

Now what, you might ask, is wrong with this? It seems reasonable enough. However, our concern is that by selling the potential idea in the first place, it sets up the wrong conditions for judging the idea. Because ideas are fragile and it is our belief that the agency and client would do better proceeding in another way.

We think that the agency should show the client all the ideas it is considering, each one of them as a line on a bit of board or paper, written simply, with no accompanying pictures or trimmings, and certainly no executional ideas to accompany them. Presenting the ideas 'naked' like this is a much purer, tougher test of an idea. It forces the agency and client to have a much deeper and more honest discussion about an idea and how and why it might work. It takes away an element of the 'sell' and it stops both parties being distracted by the execution.

Next, the agency and client should select maybe two or three potential ideas and run half-day creative workshops for each of them. If the brand idea is to run in different markets, it's vital to hold these workshops in different markets.

In these workshops the potential of a brand idea should be explored as follows. First, you should look at how you might evolve the brand idea over time, by discussing interesting avenues or ways you might express it. In effect, you'll be looking at how to evolve and sequence the idea, to create a sense of natural build and a cumulative consumer engagement. And if you've got a really good brand idea you should certainly be able to do this. This is how the Dove brand has gone to market over the last five years with 'Real Beauty is

Individual'. They've sequenced the evolution and progression of the idea very well, starting initially by seeding the idea through activation ideas and a global survey (The Dove Report), that then allowed them to evidence a much stronger point of view (Campaign for Real Beauty), that has now become more emotional in the form of the Self Esteem Foundation. So you need to ask what big messaging avenues or themes are there and how might they be sequenced.

Secondly, you should consider more detailed executional ideas; but here you should look at how the brand idea might work against specific communication tasks that could be relevant for the brand or category. For example, in the beer category a task might be: creating involvement and trial in the off-premise (supermarkets or liquor stores). Or it might be: creating behavioural loyalty. Or if this was the car category, it might be to get potential customers in for a test drive. Based on the potential brand idea, and the communication tasks in this workshop you'll then come up with executional ideas that derive from the brand idea. This kind of testing of the potential brand idea against specific communication tasks is important, because in the real world it will need to be flexible and adaptable in what it can ask consumers to do.

In the workshop there should be creative and strategic representation from both above-the-line, and below-the-line agencies, as well as the media planner. And the client should be there, but probably represented by only one or two senior individuals who ultimately will have to make the decision.

Which idea is best and why should become apparent very quickly. There will be a much deeper, rounder understanding on both client and agency side. There will be no 'sell', just real buy-in and, most important of all, the genuinely best, deepest, most interesting, most self-expanding idea will be the one that is taken forward.

If as a client, you can't find the time for these workshops, ask the agency to present two or three brand ideas in executional terms and get them to show you how the idea would develop over time by seeing it as a long corridor.

All of this really is worth it. It is so important to get this right, because the brand idea will have huge consequences for perhaps the next five years. From the client side it's vital not to rush into a decision that is based on seeing an execution or executions that you like, in one medium, particularly above-the-line, because as a 'judge', execution can play tricks on you. It sells in devious emotional ways. And from the agency side, it's important to get the right idea too. Otherwise you'll be stuck defending a 'dog' that you might only have been able to bring to life with a couple of initial executional rounds. But if that's all the idea is really capable of, the brand will be out to pitch again a couple of years later.

So as a client, you now think you've found the right brand idea. What now? Well, here again, we think there are pitfalls. It's a mistake to go 'too public, too quickly', particularly if the idea needs to work across markets. We think it's a mistake to make a big announcement internally. In other words, it is better to say, 'here is what we believe is the brand idea, now let's use it in different markets, and see what we think of it after a year'. And after a year of 'baking the idea' in different markets, we may tweak our definition. But then we will be in a position to make an announcement, that this is the official, one-and-only definition of the brand idea, bought into by all and sundry!

Consumer research

Pre-testing ads is becoming a norm. Now, we all acknowledge the dangers of over-reliance on research results. After all, everyone knows that the artificial nature of the pre-testing process means it can only be a rough guide to how consumers will react in the real world and that you can adjust an ad or a script or storyboard, solely with the purpose of improving its AI score. However, very few marketers will ignore research results, once research has been commissioned. In this day and age, when a marketer increasingly needs to justify spend, there are very few marketers who rely just on 'gut' before giving an ad the go-ahead. Instead, more and more use qualitative focus groups or rely on Millward Brown's AI scores.

And many would say that this creates safe, formulaic advertising – at just the wrong time! After all, in today's world of TV zappers, and PVRs like TiVo, what we need is communication that is, first and foremost, entertaining, and brave. So researching ads has its issues. But ads are only about 20 to 25 % of what is spent on communication as a whole. And brand ideas stretch across the whole gambit of execution. So can you pre-test a brand idea? Well of course you can. But you need to acknowledge from the outset that in creative development research, consumers will react to whatever you show them as though it's an execution. They can only really judge execution. So consumers can't judge brand ideas directly and therefore they are much harder to judge through research, than are executional ideas, or indeed, executions themselves. So if researching ads has some dangers, researching brand ideas has five times more!

When you do embark on qualitative research of a potential brand idea, your objective should be 'could this thing be made to work?' as opposed to, 'will it or won't it?' So the research should be open, and exploratory. And the skill comes in two areas. Firstly, there's a skill in how you bring a potential brand idea to life. You need to ensure there is a wide range of execution, and that this range stretches across multiple separate executional ideas. You'd probably want to insist on a minimum of ten executional ideas being brought to life. And to do this you'd use broad-brush stimuli such as: mood boards, character boards, setting boards, key visuals, concepts, other ads, etc (and not things like scripts or animatics that are more relevant for testing ads). The second area of skill involves the moderator. The moderator needs to understand completely what the client is trying to achieve, and that they are looking for the overall engagement, the sum of the parts, and not the detail.

But it's true to say that, however broad the range of execution and however good the moderator and research agency, consumers will only be able to give you feedback on how potentially engaging the execution is and the brand idea might be. They can only tell you so much. They can't tell you how self-expanding the idea is, and whether it's capable of producing three executional ideas or three hundred; and they can't tell you how connected it will be to the brand or product, and the brand/product's objectives.

The future of testing

If testing brand ideas is possible, is it actually advisable? Well, that is debatable. Many would test upstream and downstream but not test the brand idea itself – arguing that consumers can't be sensitive to the potential of a brand idea and where it could go. So upstream, they'd test insights. They'd use qualitative research to explore potential insights, before fixing on one that both resonated with consumers and could take the brand in the direction it should go, in terms of its higher order communication objectives. And then downstream, they'd research advertising ideas or activation ideas, or executions.

But they wouldn't test potential brand ideas because they'd argue that if the brand idea comes directly out of an insight and is difficult for consumers to react to, then what's the point? Our view of the matter is that if the brand idea needs to be the communication fulcrum for many years to come, then you need to research this as well. Quite simply, it's a safeguard.

But you need to do so when you've got a range of options, exposing consumers to several potential brand ideas – and not just one – because in this research you'll generally get positive feedback, if the executional stimulus is OK. So to mitigate against this 'positivism' you would want to put several potential brand ideas in front of consumers, to see which they feel is more positive. And for each of these potential brand ideas, it's vital to expose them to a broad range of potential execution. And in fact, exposing them to 'long corridors' that show how the execution will evolve over time, as described earlier, is one good way to do it.

Clients and research agencies are going to have to get good at testing brand ideas, because clients want brand ideas tested in their own right. So we've no doubt that there will be some interesting techniques developed over the next few years to do this. We might see more interactive approaches; sequential recycling approaches perhaps, a bit like how R&D departments and consumer panels interact around new product development. Another thought is that we might see research agencies talking to 'not pure consumers' but rather, a range of people like authors or scriptwriters; and with these type of people we might be able to talk to them directly about a brand idea, and to use them to explore (in their own minds or in a workshop setting), what they think they would do with one. Because people like these work with strategic types of ideas in different realms of life.

We might also see 'test labs' being used. A client could use a big shopping centre as a test lab for potential brand ideas, exposing the idea to consumers in various ways, for example, using TV screens and experiential events in foyers, and promotional signage and displays in different stores. They could then actually see the ROI from the potential idea. What a thought!

Epilogue

The era of rigorous magic

MAGICIANS LIKE HARRY KELLAR, HOWARD THURSTON and Frederick Bancroft are long forgotten, but a hundred years ago they were as famous as any modern rock god. The years 1890–1930 were the golden age of stage magic, when huge audiences packed into theatres and music halls on both sides of the Atlantic to gasp as these magicians performed tricks such as The Vanishing Birdcage and Self Decapitation. Indeed, when Harry Kellar gave his farewell performance in 1918, he was carried from the stage shoulder-high as 6,000 adoring spectators sang 'Auld Lang Syne'.

The magic that Kellar and the others practised was enabled by the latest technical innovations such as optical devices, electro-magnets and stage lighting, and refined over many hundreds of hours of painstaking rehearsal. It was un-doubtedly a rigorous process, crowned with the panache of true showmanship.

Christopher Priest's novel, *The Prestige*, tells the story of the increasingly bitter rivalry between two Victorian stage magicians, each trying to outdo the other and in it, he gives an insight into the careful way in which these tricks were staged.

Every great magic trick consists of three acts. The first act is called 'The Pledge': the magician shows you something ordinary; but, of course, it probably isn't. The second act is called 'The Turn': the magician makes this ordinary something do something extra-ordinary. Now you are looking for the secret, but you won't find it. That's why there is a third act called 'The Prestige': it's the part with the twists and turns, where lives hang in the balance and you see something shocking you've never seen before.

The three steps outlined here will be familiar to anyone who has studied the narrative structure of film, or anyone who has constructed a 30 second TVC or anyone who has planned a teaser campaign for a new product roll-out. For some of the principles of rigorous magic remain the same in any era, even though the media which deliver them may change dramatically.

Because in the early years of the twentieth century, as new entertainments like radio and cinema grew in popularity, so the allure of the stage magicians waned. And then in the 1950s, a new kind of magic came onto the scene, one driven by a single, stunning piece of technology: the television. And over the next 50 years TV held mass audiences spellbound with its dramas, sitcoms, rolling news and documentaries, not forgetting, of course, the little 30 second spots of magic in the commercial breaks. But now, the magic of TV is waning too and we believe that we are at the dawn of a new age of magic – one that brims with possibilities and energy.

In this book we've tried to analyse some of the principles on which this new rigorous magic will be based. Like the stage magic of a century ago, it will be powered by many different types of technology and it will involve all manner of ideas working together in intricate and astonishing combinations. And just as the old stage magicians would invite a member of the audience to check they had 'nothing up their sleeve' or to brave being sawn in half or impaled on a spinning knife, so this new form of rigorous magic will be participatory, engaging audiences in events, discussions, issues – even in the communication process itself. We've tried to suggest a few ways in which this is likely to happen, but the truth is that nobody can say for sure how the next stage of this rigorous magic will play out. And in trying to guess what will come next, our most useful tool may well not be research or logic or data, but, rather, the power of our imagination, because, as they say, to limit one's thoughts to facts is to limit one's hopes to possibilities.

Appendix

1. Summary: definitions of the types of ideas

Strategic ideas

Emotional platforms

Emotional platforms are emotional or cultural heartlands or territories; attempts by brands to associate themselves with an emotion or social or cultural issue to give their messages context and amplify their communications. These are the broadest type of strategic idea, but unfortunately they are often little more than glorified brand essences. They can work for some brands, but too often they lack an angle, a contradiction, or a point of view to make them really exciting and strong. They are often a precursor to the brand idea, which means that a brand usually settles on an emotional platform first, then, through interplay with execution over a number of years, stumbles on a way of sharpening it up and turning it into a brand idea.

Brand ideas

Brand ideas are the brands' point of view on the world. The best go even further, for smouldering within them is an intrinsic conflict that gives them energy and makes them very productive to work with. In short, brand ideas are half strategic and half creative, but most importantly, they are ideas that make consumers think and act in new ways.

Physical platforms

Physical platforms are physical springboards for communication such as music, film, sport, fashion or art. They are easy to work with but can be too broad, too functional and a little uninspiring. They rely on outstanding activation to carry them.

Executional ideas

Advertising ideas

These are the relatively high-level executional ideas that lie behind long-term above-the-line campaigns: the 'golden thread'. They might be a clever thought, or a character, or a relationship. Advertising ideas are not always executed above-the-line, but this will be their focus and point of origin.

Activation ideas

These are ideas in their purest sense and ones that are quite specific in their nature – they are stand-alone, one-off, bright flashes of energy in the world of marketing. They don't usually last long although they may be repeatable, but they are certainly not campaigns that last five years. And vitally, they are marketing entities that have a name, and a name the public recognise and talk about. They are participatory, and often executed through-the-line, in which case, they will tend to have an event or promotion at their centre, that is brought to life through multiple channels and disciplines.

Symbiotic ideas

Symbiotic ideas are executional ideas in which the brand message and its context directly interrelate and mutually reinforce each other. At the moment these are only really seen in the world of above-the-line. The ones that spring to mind are those with media and creative interplay. They are ideas that instantly reward the consumer, once the consumer spots the interplay and the mutual reinforcement. They run as normal ads but also as broadcast sponsorship elements.

Contextual ideas

Contextual frameworks

These are frameworks that inform when and where you communicate. They might be a few words that are about a moment, a frame of mind, a day of week or time of day, or an environment. They absolutely do not have any influence on the creative or content. So a placement strategy is a contextual idea, but as soon as the ad starts referring to its placement it becomes a symbiotic idea. Generally as a type of idea they are helpful but not that powerful or influential. They're a filter, a lens, an invisible layer. Their value comes in helping sharpen up a strategy about 'when and where' and acting as a catalyst in defining a sharp strategy articulation.

2. Fun definitions of 'an idea'

This book is all about the specialist area of communication ideas. But what about the root of all of this – ideas themselves? We all talk about ideas, a lot of the time. But have you ever tried to define an idea? It's not that easy. So we asked colleagues to tell us what they thought an idea was. We didn't find a suitable space in the book in which to use these answers, but we thought you'd be interested to read some of them nonetheless.

So here are 10 good definitions:

'The tangible expression of an original thought.'
Peter

'An idea is the defeat of habit by originality . . . my mum would say an idea is something she has (and subsequently forgets) when she's drinking red wine.'
David

'Ideas organise supposedly random, unconnected thoughts.'
John Paul

'Ideas are the way we move the world on. They are the starting point to actually doing something new. And ideas only have a value in the real world if you can and do act on them.'
Charlie

'An idea is an inspiration that emanates from the imagination and fans the flames of intentionality.'
Kirsty

'An idea is the Milky Way . . . millions of little bright lights that collectively could shine very brightly together.'
Julia

'Something original, with possibilities, future facing . . . undefined.'
Ellie

'It's a collision or contradiction of thought that holds inherent energy and interest.'
Scott

'I think an idea is . . . a thought that permits the opportunity to engage with the possible.'
Mel

'The Buddhist perspective is something like this: an idea is an action of mind that arises from karmic imprints, or the ripening of potentials within the mind, produced by past actions.'
Lawrence

References

Preface

Fielding, K. (2004) *Connection Ideas*. MEC.

Chapter 1

Earls, M. (2004) *Connection Ideas*. MEC.

Lazarus, S. (2004) *Being Magnets*. SABMiller.

Saunders, J. (2004) *Connection Ideas*. MEC.

Wieden, D. (2004) *Being Magnets*. SABMiller.

Webb Young, J. (2003) *A Technique For Producing Ideas*. NTC.

Chapter 9

Campbell, J. (1993) *The Hero With A Thousand Faces*. Paladin Books.

Grant, J. (2006) *The Brand Innovation Manifesto – How to build brands, redefine markets and defy conventions*. John Wiley & Sons, Ltd.

Chapter 10

Dru, J.-M. (2002) *Beyond Disruption*. John Wiley & Sons, Inc.

Fletcher, A. (2001) *The Art Of Looking Sideways*. Phaidon.

Foster, J. (1996) *How to Get Ideas*. Berrett-Koehler.

Grant, J. (2006) *The Brand Innovation Manifesto – How to build brands, redefine markets and defy conventions*. John Wiley & Sons, Ltd.

Webb Young J. (2003) *A Technique For Producing Ideas*. NTC.

Epilogue

Priest, C. (2005) *The Prestige*. Tor Books.

Index

Index compiled by Indexing Specialists (UK) Ltd